Actor Training 2

Actor Training 2

Brown

Wagner

Poggi

Roose-Evans

Barry

Yeaton

Richard P. Brown, editor

Institute for Acting Research with

Drama Book Specialists (Publishers)

Library of Congress Catalog Card Number: 72-90200

ISBN Book Number: 0-910482-75-6

Printed in the United States of America

CONTRIBUTORS

RICHARD BROWN is a member of the faculty at the University of California at Riverside. He is the Executive Director of the Institute for Acting Research.

ARTHUR WAGNER is Professor and Chairman of the Drama Department at the University of California, San Diego. He has founded actor training programs at Tulane University, Ohio University, Temple University and the University of California, San Diego.

JACK POGGI, an actor and teacher, is currently head of the Acting Program at C. W. Post College. He is the author of Theater in America and other works. His essay is from his forthcoming book, What Is Action?

JAMES ROOSE-EVANS, one of England's leading directors, is a specialist in experimental theatre work. He has his own workshop in London, Stage Two, and travels annually to the United States to conduct workshops for which he is famous. He is the author of Experimental Theatre and Directing a Play. The exercises described in his article belong essentially to the first phase of Stage Two's work.

PAUL BARRY founded and is Artistic Director of the New Jersey Shakespeare Festival. He has directed most of its nearly 100 productions and was named Best Director of a Play by the Drama Critics in 1973. Occasionally he acts as well. Mr. Barry teaches theatre at Drew University.

KELLY YEATON, retiring this year as head of Pennsylvania State University's Experimental Theatre, is internationally known for his publications and research in the development of arena theatre. He has been a guest director in educational and professional theatre.

If you have a piece on the training of actors, please let us know. We will send you guidelines for style.

All unsolicited manuscripts must be accompanied by a stamped self-addressed return envelope.

Mail all inquiries to:

Richard P. Brown
Executive Director
Institute for Acting Research
Department of Theatre
University of California, Riverside
Riverside, CA 92502

CONTENTS

Grateful acknowledgment is made to the Senate Research Committee of the University of California, Riverside for assistance in the preparation of this piece.

INTERIOR MONOLOGUE
AND THE ACTOR'S PRESENCE:
Some Notes on the Politics of Acting

RICHARD P. BROWN

(This piece is part of a larger work, The Politics of Acting, soon to be published by Drama Book Specialists (Publishers).)

> Many people used to believe that angels moved the stars. It now appears that they do not. As a result of this and like revelations, many people do not now believe in angels.
>
> Many people used to believe that the "seat" of the soul was somewhere in the brain. Since brains began to be opened up frequently, no one has seen "the soul." As a result of this and like revelations, many people do not now believe in the soul.
>
> Who could suppose that angels move the stars, or be so superstitious as to suppose that because one cannot see one's soul at the end of a microscope it does not exist?
>
> R. D. Laing, The Politics of Experience

HOW DO YOU DO IT?

Often, when I am doing workshops and demonstrations on sub-text and Interior Monologue around the country, colleagues ask: "Where did this come from? How did you get to this?"

Where does any of our work come from; any work? Is it total-ly new? It's hard to say. Those of us whose main work is with ac-tors -- in training programs, workshops or productions -- have (it seems to me) stopped caring about origins finally. Mostly, it comes down to something like the story that the fine theorist Elder Olson told when asked if writers themselves talked about the theory and technique of writing structure, about poetics. "In a way," he said, "Dylan Thomas used to slam his hand against his head and say very loudly: 'How the hell did he do it? How the hell did Willy Yeats do it?!'"

Sometimes you can tell something about your "genesis" of a particular part of your particular work. Mostly you try to figure out how to do it. Later (sometimes) comes the theory, the "why it happened the way it did" part. It is a very interesting part and, by far, the safest. Hindsight covers our mistakes. I once marveled at a show of color work that a photographer friend had done and said to him: "How do you do it? How do you come up with such terrific stuff so consistently?" "Easy," he told me, "I throw out nineteen of every twenty shots I do and show you what's left." Easy.

One has to be very careful about telling stories about how this or that piece of the work came about. Sooner or later they all be-gin to sound like something out of a matched set of Elbert Hubbard: "I was sitting in my kitchen one morning..."

On the other hand, you can't just say: "Grotowski made me do it." Or Joe or Bill or Richard. Who's going to buy that?

So: I was sitting in my kitchen one morning...

THE BACKGROUND

Some years ago I was working on a project with a young play-wright and a young director, a production of a new and challenging script called The Gift. As rehearsals progressed, it became clear that both Hurst Rinehart, the director, and the actors were having difficulty with the particular nature of the text. The plot action was fairly straightforward. A young married man encounters another young man at a bus station and brings him home to the apartment in which he and his wife live. The husband offers the young man shel-ter for an indeterminate length of time. In short order the visitor becomes involved with the wife in a sado-masochistic sexual rela-tionship. The husband is reduced to a kind of servant/spectator in the course of the relationship between the wife and the visitor.

2

Finally, it is clear to both the husband and wife that the young man has fulfilled his role in the scenario and the young man leaves. There are obvious similarities between this structure and that of Pinter's plays, and a number of the difficulties which confront actors and directors in dealing with a Pinter text were also present in this circumstance.

On one hand, the events which transpired were clear enough, but, on the other hand, the nature of those events on an interpersonal and existential, moment-by-moment basis was difficult for both the actors and director to pin down. This was not just a question of motivation, but of the actual taste or flavor of the moments as they were experienced by the characters and perceived by the audience. As an intentional device of the writing technique, the author had placed a barrier between the text and the subtext. This screen varied from somewhat translucent to completely opaque. At the suggestion of the playwright, the director began working with the actors in an effort to arrive at choices which would invest the text in its playing with sufficient energy and momentum that the events represented would have the kind of surface tension and dynamic which he felt implicit in this theatrical mode. When I began to work with the company, it was apparent to me that the problem was one of developing a sufficiently clear and direct subtext so that the elements of the action could be played in such a way as to carry a charge of immediate experience without fracturing the opacity of the playwright's text.

The director had already worked with the actors in defining a series of possible motivations for each of the units of action in the text, but the motivational definition did not seem to carry sufficient strength in the playing to energize the opaque text. The decisions remained largely intellectual on the part of the actors -- not interiorized enough to achieve a strong dynamic in the playing. The events had no specific and discernable flavor.

Most of the questions which had been asked in building a motivational pattern were the traditional ones: "What does the character want?" "Why is he/she doing this?" -- the entire cluster of motivational, unit-analysis tools left us in the Stanislavsky heritage. The trouble was that none of it was working.

The actors could discuss, and at some length, each of the possibilities for "motivating" a particular event, but these discussions and the decisions which grew out of them never seemed to carry over into the playing of the text. The characters lacked any real life. The actors, in short, could not find a way to be present in the action in such a way as to inform it.

This is not an uncommon difficulty with young and somewhat inexperienced actors and not unknown even with trained professionals at times. Most actors of any intellectual capacity at all are able with minimal guidance to arrive at a motivational unit analysis of a text.

The problems encountered here were, of course, aggravated by the fact that the text gave no clear map of the decisions which needed to be made. That is, the patterns of action were not causally connected in any observable way to the motivations which underlay them. To put it somewhat differently, the logic of motivation which is apparent in most realistic texts, which allows an actor to reason backward from the pattern of action to what must have preceded it motivationally, was absent in this particular script.

Where was it in the text that the character revealed what he/she was up to and what was "going on" on a moment-to-moment basis? The text offered no answers, and both the playwright and the director were interested in pursuing methods by which one could deal with the existential and phenomenological problems of opacity in human action. We wished to avoid, if we could do it, an "explication" of the motivational patterns of the play.

One day, after many false starts and very little success, one of the actors complained bitterly, "This is like trying to play the action of a Joyce novel with everything but the bare events left out!" As it happened, I had been reading Virginia Woolf and the remark struck me. It seemed to me that what Woolf and Joyce had been up to, in part, was the creation of a tangible projection of what Stanislavsky had called the subtext of an action. They had constructed in their fiction a way of showing "what is going on," the root system of the existential moment.

This notion led me to suggest that in our work we do the same thing for the moments in the text: expand the time sequence so as to allow room for the actors to explore the "events" which comprised the life of the moment toward which the lines of the text pointed. The lines, we decided, could be treated as the signal flags flown by the characters in extremis, or as a map of the territory of the action.

After considerable struggle to develop the rules of the game, we found ourselves able to penetrate into a moment by taking notice of the particles or events in flux inside and between the characters and arrive at decisions about the nature of a productive subtextual framework.

The rules, finally, were very simple ones. Each actor began to verbalize and vocalize (and, as a by-product, to physicalize) the component events of each moment. Rather than the usual action-reaction chain, with its separate links, the time -- now stretched out to its inclusive limits -- assumed the broad dimension of simultaneous and related life events with all the characters acting and reacting at the same time. All of us could hear what was "going on" within and between the people of the play.

The actors were at first troubled by their own tendency to make prior (and usually over-simplified) decisions about what they were going "to do," very much in the way that actors beginning to work in theatre games are plagued by performing and playwriting. A lot of work on games and their discipline of <u>doing</u> overcame this difficulty.

Now we had a multiple track and very tangible subtext interwoven of the experiential layers of the characters. "Say what is going on," the actors were told. Questions, lots of them.

What do I hear?

What do I see?

How do I feel about it?

What do I think is happening?

What do I wish were happening?

What do I think he/she is seeing, hearing, feeling, wanting?

What does this make me remember?

What response am I getting?

What shall I do to get the response I want?

What is the environment doing to me?

What are my hands feeling, my feet, my neck, my groin?

How much of all this is showing? How much should?

What is my cover? How does it make me feel?

And a lot more.

We found that there were things happening -- events, memories and fantasies that were conditioning the moments -- not available to the character but needed by the actor. We framed questions which reporduced the process of feeling and perception followed by the operations of denial, forgetting, projection and so forth which raised the element and then buried it. Operations which were at work in a moment but unnoticed by the character were explored and made specific and concrete, put into a form that the actor could use. Questions were the main element of side coaching, narrowing down to parts of the body, widening to memory, association and fantasy. They led us to an abundance of material used to provide the bedrock of the characters' common "now." There it all was; we could all see it and hear it. The playwright took notes, rewrote lines, even whole scenes.

There was too much and a lot of it was wrong for what we wanted to do. But now there was a way to pick and arrange, to score the subtext, to pare away the excess, to focus on particular aspects, to change the elements of any moment. We had options. We had begun to arrive at a way of working which met the primary need for the actors' approach to presence in a given existential moment on the stage: "Do it now, then fix what was wrong." We found that we could score scenes by forming shared patterns of focus. When we emphasized body awareness, we got one kind of scene; when we emphasized associations and memory, we got another kind. Balance and focus could be shared and dealt with.

We found it easy to fix things. When an actor was having trouble with a particular moment, we could look at what he/she was using in the subtext, examine what was included, what excluded, what emphasized and discover with a great deal of specificity what should or could be added or omitted to make the moment work better.

In this rather crude way the method I have called interior monologue (with a bow to Woolf) began to take shape for me. It is clear that the idea of subtext is neither new nor especially revolutionary. What was revealing to all of us who worked on that first project was that the interior monologue gave us a way of joining analysis to playing; the very act of working through a text in the now of playing it. The actors had a series of steps which they could take "on the floor" which, at the same time that it opened up the text for them on a visceral level, revealed the nature of their own working process at any given moment.

After a time it was possible to drop the vocalization of the interior monologue while continuing to touch all the points which the vocalization had shown us. It then became possible to allow some of the verbalization to drop back to other modes of knowing within the person (actor) and still retain the score which had been arrived at in the first level of work. At any time when it seemed that there was a loss of specificity, we went back into vocalization to explore "what was going on."

We learned a number of important things about the process of working and scoring the subtext:

1. Verbalization forces specific experiences into concrete, though not always "coherent" or "logical" form. A lot of the vocalized material was not in the form of sentences; often they were flashes of impressions: colors, sensations, partially stated sensations, memories and the like. No attempt was made to force the "events" into the mold of grammar.

2. Vocalizations force an opening up of time and of the multi-layered sets which precede the overt "action" of a piece. The text emerges as a kind of topographical map of experience with the same sort of relation to the actual, felt experience of playing as a topographical map of a geographic area has to the experienced landscape. One can navigate by it, but not live in it.

3. Once actors have trained themselves in the exploration of the subtextual terrain by vocalization, they can learn to do the same thing, cover the same topography, with great speed, dropping vocalization and verbalization. The same process of specification of experience, the taste of the actual, remains.

4. By dis/covering the elements of a particular moment, it is often possible to dis/cover where actors are censoring, avoiding a part of the landscape of the moment in which the characters find themselves. At these times it becomes necessary to do other work to bring the actor's territory more into line with that of the character. These problems, of course, are close to the heart of the political dimensions of the acting process: to all of those questions of what we allow ourselves to see, hear, feel or even think about. The rules of this allowing are common to both the character and the actor and need extensive work. When the politics can't be dealt with in rehearsal, we found that the Interior Monologue gave us a way to shape a path around a block in the actors' territories and achieve something close to what we knew was the ideally right score.

5. Where the textual "map" is open -- either unclear or unspecific about what the subtextual events might be -- one need not, we found, argue about "interpretation," but try, operationally, to arrive at a productive series of choices -- assumptions, working hypotheses -- which lead into the overall action of the piece rather than out of it. "Is the character angry here because of what has just happened (been said, guessed at, etc., whatever)?" The text doesn't give a hint. Compare where "yes" leads as opposed to where "no" leads -- in terms, not only of this moment or cluster of moments, but in terms of the overall shape of the piece.

6. The shape of the score of the subtext can be made very concrete so that consistency, the ability of the actors, individually and jointly, to repeat what they have done, is not difficult to achieve; but if the I M is played through each time, the score will never be identical twice. The actor will, in fact, be "doing it" each time as a slightly different person with slightly different "others" in a slightly different place; growth within the score is maintained.

7. Playing is itself a multilayered event. There are several levels on which "what is going on" is an important question: the character's level; the level of the character "in relation" to all of the "others" of the character's life; the level of the actor; the actor "in relation" to all of the "others" who constitute the present of preparation, training, development of pieces; and the presentation for witnesses. All of the rules of these levels, the politics of acting, are so closely linked that we ignore them at our peril. (My discussion of the political dimensions of working with actors is based on the insights and published work of R. D. Laing.)

8. There is an important and inescapable difference between acting and therapy: the actor has no option not to dis/cover. The politics of the person is subject to the discipline of the art.

9. There are a lot of ways to get to the same place.

WHAT THEN?

What has occurred since that first exploration has been largely a series of confrontations with questions that arise out of the use of I M in a variety of different circumstances of training, preparation and performance. The question, "What is going on?" is at the same time useful and frustrating. It means quite different things in the differing context of differing styles of writing and playing, for instance. Comedy has a very different subtextual dimension than serious works. And the shape of the subtext in Pinter is a world away from that in Brecht. In direct performance, such as Grotowski's, the I M of the text is a parallel terrain to the I M of the performer and that relationship must be worked out very carefully.
The political questions are the most difficult. "What is going

on?" is a personal question in our context; not surprising, because the theatre is finally an art of persons in relation. It relates, as we discovered in our first project, not only to a single character, but to fabrics of characters; to their presented selves, in Irving Goffman's phrase (Goffman, 1959); to their ego states, as Eric Berne has laid them out for us (Berne, 1961); and for the political knots which R. D. Laing describes in his work (see, eg., 1960). All of these questions are tied closely to the political considerations of the actor's use of his/her body and voice (see, eg. Lowen, 1967 and Feldenkrais, 1972). And they relate strongly to the cultural politics of our world -- who is and who is not permitted to enter "extraordinary states of being" like those of the actor (see Szasz, 1970 for instance).

All of the people: characters, actors, teachers, directors and witnesses are people in relation. On each of the levels of relation the search for "what is going on" takes on important weight. Acting, teaching, directing, witnessing: all of these are involved with some sort of intervention by those who are in relation to each other's lives. This intervention is, in fact, the material out of which we make and respond to the theatre.

The terminology, the words we use to describe these interventions, are not very important, but the processes by which we relate are important. The scenarios of these interventions, whether in the relation of Willy Loman to Biff or in the relation of the actors playing these roles to each other as artists/people, follow human and highly personal forms. Whether we are dealing with human experience indirectly on the stage (as in the presentation of a text piece) or directly, when the performer (as in Grotowski's theatre) relates to a "role" as a person to a territory in which he dis/covers himself/herself, in each case the actor is a person with one or more personae laid on, and present in the presence of witnesses who experience him/her while he/she is experiencing. Public solitude. Dis/covery.

WHAT NOW?

The scope of this paper is too small to delve very deeply into the realm of politics of acting, the whole fabric of rules and rule-making which govern the acting process -- the questions of how, when, where and under what conditions the experience of dis/covery appears to happen. I would like here to spread out only a few of the ideas which seem to me important in exploring the area.

1.   There are several layers to the political dimensions of what

9

actors do -- from the training period through performance. All of these layers are bound up in the fact that the theatre is the most interpersonal of the arts; it functions as a complex series of relationships between living people. The acting performance on the stage consists of a person doing something in the presence of other persons -- not _for_ them, but _before_ them. The directing process consists of defining the territory of the total performance, the shaping and scoring of the general experience of a group of witnesses who, during the rehearsal process are not present, but "given." The training process consists, usually, of a teacher putting himself/ herself in relation to an actor in such a way that the actor will be able to enter a performance territory and deal with it. On each of these levels, the keystone of the work is the relationship of the persons to each other as persons. When we scratch away the divergences of terminology, all of the approaches to acting that I know of aim at making it possible for persons to share experience, either determinate (matrixed) or non-determinate (scored at the moment of presentation).

2.   In performance there are several time lines operating. In realistic, scripted performance, for instance, there are three primary time lines operating: that of the actor in his/her own person, that of the "character," and that of the audience. The actor's time line and the audience's time line are identical in one sense: they occupy the same time span on the clock from the moment each enters the performance time/space. The time line of the "character" is broken and shaped in most performances (except those in which all characters are present in the space for the entire time of the performance, in those rare cases where nothing is omitted from the stage which occurs in the time line of the "characters"). For the most part, both actors and audience are concerned primarily with a time line which is a product of all three of the above: it is the time line of the performance. Looked at in this way, it seems that all of the elements of the personal side of performance focus on the interaction of the time lines of actors, audience and "character" within the performance time/space. The audience's time line needs to be dealt with, for instance, not only as a communal line, but also as a collection of individual ones.

There are questions always hovering in the performance time/ space which are operative in the performance time line. How full and how empty is the house? What are the rules governing responses of audience to performance -- signs of approval or disapproval, permission to engage in other activities such as talking, eating and so forth, permission for witnesses to move about, either moving into the performance time line or out of it into some activity unrelated to the performance (as in the Oriental theatre)? These and many other questions will have a strong and direct bearing on the actor's time line of experience and behavior and also on the nature of the performance time line as it was originally conceived and as it exists on a particular day.

Both the collaboration of performers and director in preparing the performance and the training of actors and directors deal largely with a craft of manipulating the human dimension of these time lines. Directors are trained to score the Hamlet/Ghost scene in such a way that it will be a different kind of experience from the Hamlet/Polonius scene. Actors are trained to make such a difference possible in the creation of their performance time lines. And both are trained to deal with the divergences of the audience time lines.

For the actors, the most important part of the work is creating a viable relationship between their personal time lines with those of the "character" time lines. Since it is finally the actor who is experienced by the audience, the heart of the actor's problem as a human being/artist is to create a way of dealing with all of the rule-making procedures which go into making the performance possible: the rule-making relationship to himself/herself, to the figure (present or imagined), his/her director, his/her audience and all of the possible combinations of these. The craft is a craft of coping with these relationships in such a way that performance is possible and as good as these particular individuals can make it at the moment of its happening.

3.   I suspect that our strongest tool in dealing with the politics of training is to move the emphasis in the work from understanding to doing and experiencing. In making this shift we will have to come to grips with the hyper-intellectual quality of much of our supposedly studio work. When we are working with actors on a subtext, for instance, we will have to provide conditions in which noticing is of essential importance. Most actors do not omit or censor elements from the subtext because they do not understand them or because they are incapable in any absolute sense of imagining them. My experience is that where the actor does not provide for the fullness of the landscape of events which constitute the territory of the character, it is usually because there is some rule operating in the territory of the actor which will not allow that particular element to be employed in the creation of an analog in the territory of the character.

Using the technique of the vocalized Interior Monologue is only a first step in filling in the character territory from the resources of the actor's territory. It provides the actor only with the knowledge that an element is being censored, not with the means of dealing with the rule which prohibits that element from being accessible to him/her.

Great care must be exercised at this point. There is no such

thing as too much caution here. It doesn't take a genius to understand what is being censored. Either the element is left out of the
I M entirely or there is a quick and marked loss of power, "voltage,"
when that element is reached. "Aha!," proclaims the teacher,
"See, you're censoring out (insert your favorite actor omission
here)! Let us examine the roots of that. Tell me about your (insert your favorite confession here)." It cannot be stressed too strongly that the rule, deeply imbedded in the actor, is as potent as at the
moment of its formation, and the teacher or director who meddles
carelessly with the actor's psychic landscape is in for a lot of trouble.
It is possible to work on blocks, but the work must be done very carefully.

The goal of the work in this area is to make it possible for
elements of the actor's territory to become increasingly accessible and usable in the creation of fictional territories, but to make
such access necessary is to impose an additional rule which conflicts with the original and still very potent rule against such access
and risks serious damage to the actor as well as raising the possibility that a double bind of conflicting injunctions will make acting
seem an impossible task, not to say an unbearably painful one.

There is no need to discuss particular exercises at this point;
all exercises are only as useful as the impulse which guides their
use, and any impulse which sets the actor against himself/herself,
which starts from the rule, "You must...," is potentially very destructive.

When actor territory is the problem, what is needed is a kind
of work which allows the person to notice limitation in the territory
and to find ways for himself/herself to defuse the inhibiting rule or
(and this happens very often) to make another choice which comes
close to what is needed. All of this work must be self-limiting, it
must contain a way out for those who need it; and no one can decide
for another when or whether it is needed. I don't believe that any
teacher or director who is not a professionally trained therapist
should set an actor on a path on which he/she must overthrow a rule
deeply imbedded in his/her territory "OR ELSE."

Happily, work which focuses on noticing, on awareness free
of pressure, can defuse the large proportion of those actor territory problems which we face. Noticing doesn't require solutions in
public. The great strength of theatre games as a technique of working is that they place the emphasis on an open-ended game problem
with many solutions and with usable craft as a by-product. Even
here, however, there is the danger that facility with game strategy
(not necessarily the same as acting talent) may assume an inordinate-
ly important dimension and implant as potent a rule of achievement
and self-evaluation as the personal rule it seeks to overcome.

12

4.   We need, as teachers and directors, to stop dealing with students on the basis of inherited or appropriated techniques which are limited to mechanical <u>procedures,</u> a series of exercises employed with no human impulse behind them; even a set of "concepts" can, when robbed of their humanity, become manipulative tools. Procedures merely accelerate the tendency in our culture to reify human beings, to turn them into things <u>to which</u> and <u>with which</u> we can do wonderful things, great workshops, spectacular productions. We need to look for ways to reverse the trend of the culture's push to make us think of even ourselves as things, organisms, quanta. Particularly in the theatre, the person is primary. We cannot approach the theatre split into mind and body, psyche and soma, intelligence and instrument. As long as we continue to tacitly buy the notion in our work that we are fundamentally and essentially a collocation of bones, muscles, nerves and the like, we can never approach the problems of action and character (or non-character) or the newer problems of direct performance, non-matrixed performance and so forth; because these things have humanity, the presumption of personhood, at their center. The rule making, the rule breaking, the self awareness that makes human art possible are irrelevant to things; the politics of performance is meaningless in any but an art of persons.

Psychology, anthropology and sociology are beginning now to look at us as a world of persons. Workers in these fields are rejecting the view of the world as a collection of things to be counted, patterned, searched for pathology, diagnosed, treated, engineered, solved, repaired, junked. Basic questions that have been important in the theatre since its beginning -- What is a human action? How do actions relate? What has morality to do with states of being?-- these and many others are being given serious study. Often the theatre itself, in its most humane form, is the analog for theoretical models (see, eg., Goffman, 1959). There is much to learn about our most important questions, especially from those who have no vested interest in our institutionalized theatre.

5.   One of the areas which needs most work is the relationship between effort, awareness (or noticing) and performance. The problem of getting an actor to "let it happen" is an old and very troublesome one. My experience is that the more goal-oriented, achievement-oriented an actor becomes, the less likely he/she is to do a good job at being present in the work. One example of this sort of difficulty, drawn from the area of the actor's relation to his/her own politics as it relates to the politics of the character, may illustrate something of what we are up against.

If we take three modes of experience: imagination, memory and perception, it is clear that while all three may occur at the same time, a person may be more "in touch" with one or the other of these modes of his/her experience at any given time. The degree to which one loses awareness of the operation of the other modes in which he/she is experiencing might be thought of as unconscious experience. Laing put it this way: "The unconscious is what we do not communicate to ourselves or to one another." (Laing, 1961, p. 17). Still, someone else might be aware that something is "going on" in the person, even though he/she may not know specifically what it is. Depending on how that outside person reacts to the "something going on," it may become an important operative element in what happens between the two people. Jack has a residue of hostility left from a previous event. The residue has been pushed down from his awareness; he doesn't notice it. Jill notices something in Jack which she takes to mean that he is feeling hostile towards her and reacts accordingly, by withdrawing (say). Jack notices her withdrawal and reacts. And so forth into a spiral. If one adds a witness to this situation, we have the basis of a theatrical performance.

On the actor's side, anxiety about the performance he/she is doing might spring from memory of past failures projected on to the present and experienced as worry about the future, so that the doing is robbed of energy in the present. If a strong sense of awareness, of noticing, is included in the craft preparation of actors, the swings between modes of experience might be noticed; they might well be defused and the actor's energy be brought quickly back to the moment of doing in performance.

There is another reason why awareness of mode swings is important to actors. Characters in realistic plays are subject to a circularity of such swings and actors need to duplicate the condition of characters who are suffering from them. For instance: Willy Loman -- looking at his poor little yard, remembering the past, imagining the future, comparing that imagined future to his remembered imaginings of it and erupting with tremendous force back into the present -- "How can they whip cheese!" If the actor can deal with such mode swings (he/she doesn't have to deal with the concept, but with the experience) he/she is equipped to handle some of the most potent kinds of revelations of the human condition of which the theatre is capable.

6.   Much work needs to be done in what we loosely call "relaxation." Most of us are aware of how self-defeating the injunction "Relax!" is. It is an automatic double bind, a set of contrary injunctions. We can not relax in any real sense in response to a command, no matter how mildly stated. The pattern of injunctions of this kind are extremely strong in our culture. (See Laing, 1959). We even have jokes about it

14

"You will enjoy yourself, or else. "

Most of the "relaxation" work I have seen operates on this "or else" level. The additional energy generated by the "or else" portion of the rules and injunctions which we internalize (introject) and integrate into our life scripts may, some researchers think, become stored in the physical part of our selves, in the nerves and muscles, in habits of holding things physically inside ourselves. (See Lowen, 1967.) In the theatre we recognize the surplus energy as "indicating, " using excessive effort in realizing an event -- ranging from exaggerated walking, sitting and so forth to outright mugging. I have come to think that the energy is the carrier medium for attitudes to be conveyed, "illustrating rather than doing." Energy of this sort, attached to, but not a functional part of an event seems to me largely an attitudinal spillover, a judgmental impulse which is accreted to the primary impulse, a sort of meta-impulse.

Meta-impulses disturb performance in other ways too. We have all seen actors try something they have been asked to do, and seen that often the main message which comes singing through is: "I can't do this. See how bad I am." And on and on. These accreted impulses tend to magnify the primary feeling surrounding an event; they are the "O My God..." fastened to the primary impulse. Meta-impulses are, in my experience, the sure sign of an overactive judgmental function in the actor and can wreck a performance or even a studio exercise. They create an immobilizing hysteria in which the primary focus of awareness -- on the thing to be done -- is lost and shifted to the meta-impulse of judgment. The result is often indication or actor comment of some sort.

We need to find ways of achieving relaxation which ties noticing to acceptance. I have found meditation techniques very useful in approaching the problem, but anything which will promote ease, "centering" or "finding the still point" would work. I do not believe that superficial muscular "relaxation" will do any more than leave the actor confused and distressed about why he/she is still feeling internally agitated and as clattery as a dropped tray of tin cups when he/she has "become a pool of jelly" on the studio floor (teacher crooning low in the background about sandy beaches). Clatter, clatter.

7. Somehow we need to find a way to deal with the primary politics of the teaching of acting so as to divest ourselves of the comforting mantle of parent cum guru, dispensing palliative catch phrases like aspirin in a welfare clinic. If our goal is to prepare our actors to be independent artists, there is little chance that we can do it by pretending to be sages while acting like parents sprinkling approval or disdain as reward and punishment. This is violence of the worst and most destructive sort. Teaching acting is an intense sort of human interaction, filled with the same pitfalls that await the therapist:

transference, counter-transference and all the rest. The temptation to be other than we are, to pose as the holders of truth, of a "way" to which others must aspire (all the while denying it) or perish is very great. Too often, though, as Laing has put it: "We are effectively destroying ourselves by violence masquerading as love." (1975, p. 50.)

8.   We need to help each other in ways that we haven't begun to dream of.

References

Berne, Eric (1961). Transactional Analysis in Psychotherapy: A Systematic Individual and Social Psychiatry. New York: Grove Press.

Feldenkrais, Moshe (1972). Awareness Through Movement. New York: Harper and Row.

Goffman, Erving (1959). The Presentation of Self in Everyday Life. Garden City: Doubleday Anchor Books.

Laing, R. D. (1960). The Divided Self. London: Tavistock Publications. Page citations are from the Pelican Books edition (1965) London: Penguin Books.

Lowen, Alexander (c. 1967). The Betrayal of the Body. New York: Collier Books.

Szasz, Thomas S. (c. 1970). Ideology and Insanity. Garden City: Anchor Books.

ERIC BERNE, T. A., AND
THE ACTOR'S TEXT ANALYSIS

ARTHUR WAGNER

One of the primary tasks of any acting system, method, process, or what-have-you is to provide the actor with tools that aid in making choices concering character and action with confidence, which stimulate the actor's intuition. Some of us tend to be suspicious of the word "intuition" because of its reference to the "intuitive" actor whose only tool may be what he refers to as intuition: intuition as a priori, sui generis, fait accompli, an end in itself and self sufficient. The "intuitive" actor assumes that all he needs is a good reading of the play, some props and other actors; his "natural" talent (read intuition) will do the rest.

I suggest that the intuition is a good deal more complex and that the actor must have a barrage of weapons in order to penetrate the intuition's unknown and juiciest resources. Isn't that what Stanislavsky did? My own work with Eric Berne's transactional analysis system has made me even more aware and sensitive to this particular aspect of the actor's process. The theory of transactional analysis is one of the most useful tools available for providing the young actor with confidence-building choices that stimulate the actor's intuition.

It is not my intention in this short paper to delve into the implications and functions of confidence and intuition, but a short digression on these two elements would be helpful. Curiously, Berne's initial theoretical discoveries were made as a result of his interest in intuition and are the main concern of his first T. A. articles. As for confidence, it frees. We stretch the voices and the bodies of our young actors so that they may have confidence that their instruments can do more than just play the notes -- that they can play them well and with variety. Without that confidence the actor will not risk, no more than a singer will go for that high C, without the technique to achieve it. So much for "formal" risks. What about content, guts, the emotions, the power of the inner life? Will actors risk in those areas without confidence in their choices for that kind of exposure? Not likely. They'll play dead, lie doggo, play safe. But if they are

19

confident in their choices, then they will open themselves to their implications, take the risk, and thereby allow their intuition to be stimulated.

Transactional analysis is a codified and organized theory of social behavior, understandable to the layman. It uses vernacular language that strikes directly to the intuition. As a result, actors who can use it are provided with myriad sources for making choices about the inner lives of the characters they play; they have an organized check-list of things to look for, to make decisions about, which allow them to work in great detail, in depth and with richness. The text analysis concerns itself with the immediate score of a given situation (the moment-to-moment actions and objectives) as well as all the antecedent materials needed to justify that immediate score. This analysis is broken down into three analytical components: structure analysis, transaction analysis and script analysis. The following is a sample check-list of T. A. categories -- guideposts for a detailed character text analysis.

I. Structure Analysis

The topology of the individual personality in its component parts has mainly to do with ego states and their function in a particular individual. There are universal constants about ego states which help identify them. The four criteria for determining ego states are voice, gesture, demeanor and vocabulary. It was this concept which first led me to a deeper examination of the implications of T. A. The vocabulary is provided by the playwright while the actor provides the content supporting the vocabulary through the external expression of voice, gesture and demeanor. Since there are three ego states (see below), there are hints not only to the inner life of the character, but also to the external manifestation of that life through not one voice for his character, but three. Below is the check-list for a structural analysis:

A. Ego States: coherent systems of thought and feelings manifested by corresponding patterns of behavior (Berne).
 1. Parent
    critical
    nurturing
 2. Adult
    data processing
 3. Child
    natural
    adapted (influenced by Parent)

B. Shifts in Ego States: the shift of psychic energy from one ego state to another.

1. Boundaries rigid or flexible
2. Which states most readily cathected (energized)
3. Executive power of ego state
4. "Real" self

C. Psychopathology of Ego States (anomalies of psychic structure)
    1. Exclusion (one or two ego states never cathected)
    2. Contamination (one ego state contaminating another)

II. Transaction Analysis

Each individual needs to structure his time from birth to death. Theatre pieces are structured to show characters in the process of social transaction and, in rare cases, the lack of social transaction. A transaction is defined as a unit of social intercourse that involves a stimulus and response. Each stimulus has the potential of eliciting a response from any one of the ego states of the receiver, creating a decision to be made by the actor. Each transaction is a unit in a time structure (see below), all of which yield one or more of four different kinds of advantages: psychological, social, biological and existential. Advantages are analogous to, and supportive of, the character's objectives.

A. Transactions
    1. Complementary
    2. Crossed
    3. Simple
    4. Duplex (ulterior)

B. Time Structures
    1. Withdrawal (lack of social transaction, i. e., a soliloquy)
    2. Ritual (stylized exchanges; strokes; greetings and leavings)
    3. Activities (work; not found often in theatre pieces)
    4. Pastimes (chit chat; minimally in theatre pieces; the bulk of Waiting for Godot)
    5. Games (angular and duplex transactions with a "gimmick"; mutual payoff; conscious transaction; a maneuver game; prevalent transactions of theatre pieces)
    6. Intimacy (game free; giving and receiving without exploitation; infrequent but potent moments in theatre pieces)

Transactions and time structures are all-inclusive. The four kinds of transactions and six time structures cover every possible example in real or play life, although the variety of combinations, especially in games, is multiple enough to satisfy anyone's need for individuality.

III. Script Analysis

In his book What Do You Say After You Say Hello? Berne defined a script as follows: "An ongoing program, developed in early childhood under parental influence, which directs the individual's behavior in the most important aspects of his life." For the first time he also defined non-script: "Non-script would then be reversible behavior, with no particular time schedule, developed later in life, and not under parental influence. This is a fairly good description of autonomy, which is, in fact, the opposite of script." The latter kind of situation would be rarely found in theatre pieces. Who would want to see Hamlet autonomous; that is, after therapy? The last thing the actor wants to do is make his character well. So we can plunge ahead and look for the character's script and find that, like a play, it has a beginning, middle and end; crises and climaxes; and may have a happy or tragic ending.

The script check-list below provides the actor with all the information necessary for creating both the subjective and objective biography of his character. The subjective biography contains all the information the character would consciously know about himself, while the objective biography contains all the information which the character does not consciously know but which the actor needs to know about his character in order to play organically. I firmly believe that the more details the actor has put into his "bag" and head, the greater his belief in his role. The conclusions the actor draws about his character from the script check-list are as follows:

A. Life course (Parental injunction from parent's Child; super objective)
B. Counter life course (from parent's Parent)
C. Position (I'm okay, You're okay, etc.)
D. Decision (one phrase or sentence which reveals character's attitude about self or others)
E. Favorite games
F. Sweatshirt (persona character presents to the world)
G. Trading stamps collected
H. Racket (the way in which one collects trading stamps)
I. Mythical hero
J. Physiological component (which sphincter is uptight?)

In order to make decisions about the check-list items, the actor might ask such questions as these:

What are your parents like?

Whom were you named after?

Who named you?

Did you have any nicknames?

What was your favorite fairy tale as a child?

What kinds of feelings bother you most?

What did your parents talk about at the dinner table?

Where will you be five years from now, if all goes well?

Where will you be five years from now, if all goes badly?

What would you put on your sweatshirt so people would know it was you coming?

How long are you going to live?

What will they put on your tombstone?

Are you a winner or a loser? A non-winner?

Do you have any sexual hang-ups?

What do the voices in your head tell you?

Do you have hallucinations?

Where do your OK words come from ?

What is your metaphor scene?

What are your security phrases?

What is your gallows transaction?

This is only a partial list of Berne's condensed list. His full script check-list has 220 questions. Actors must choose those that are most meaningful to them and which refer most specifically to the character in question. Obviously the list will vary with different characters.

SECOND THOUGHTS ON THE THEORY OF ACTION

JACK POGGI

Stanislavsky's theory of "action" has taken deep root in America and pervaded the thinking of many actors and directors. For years I held to the theory myself, but I have had to let go of it, partly because it failed to answer some nagging questions in my mind, partly because I was often unhappy with the results when I saw it put into practice. *

One reason why the theory is widely accepted is that it contains within it a profound truth. Stanislavsky often told his actors, "Never mind about feeling, act and the feeling will come." It was one of his many striking insights. He saw clearly that the actor cannot play "anger," for example, but I think he was never quite precise about what the actor plays instead. He gave as an example, "to get even with my enemy." That would be an "action." But the verb "to get even" describes only the end result to be attained, it does not describe what the character does in order to get even.

Stanislavsky tried to get around the difficulty by breaking actions down into small units: for example, "to slap my enemy's face." Clearly that is something you can do, a simple physical activity. But what do you do with words? What is it exactly that you do with a speech in iambic pentameter that leads your enemy to believe that his wife is sleeping with his lieutenant? Is your action "to get him to believe it"? If you put it that way you are right back to describing the result you want to bring about, and you still have not said what you do in order that he will believe it. The examples of verbal actions commonly offered by Stanislavsky and his followers seem to me to describe what the character wants, not what he does. In America, in fact, the term "action" is frequently synonomous with "purpose" or "objective."

---

*Mira Rostova helped me to see exactly what was wrong with the action theory and taught me a useful alternative.

Stanislavsky never intended that. He used the Russian word deistvie, which suggests movement or process, not objective. He saw that there was a difference between the two, but to my mind he never clarified it satisfactorily. In reading him I sometimes feel that by "action" he meant a kind of immediate objective on the way to the achievement of some more distant goal. Perhaps this is because of his emphasis on the "super-objective," the ultimate goal to which all the actions and objectives of the character are supposed to be directed. Stanislavsky seemed to think that characters in plays are always striving for something beyond what can be achieved at the moment, and that the pattern of the struggle could be sketched out like the "spine" of a fish, with all the little purposes feeding into larger ones.

I find all this very dubious, both as psychology and dramaturgy, but that is not my main concern. I also find that the attempt to put Stanislavsky's theory into practice (at least as I have seen it in America) frequently leads the actor astray. A great many American actors have got it firmly fixed in their heads that, no matter what role they play, they must always choose a goal of some kind and pursue it pell-mell. There is hardly a beginning class in improvisation in which the following situation, or something very like it, is not given to the students. One student is told that he needs ten dollars desperately and that he must get it from his roommate; another is told that he needs the money himself and is on his way out of the room. Each student is told to "play your action" as vigorously as possible, stopping at nothing. Such improvisations are often fun to do. The students get caught up in the problem, and if they are inventive they come up with some ingenious tactics. If both pursue their goals unrelentingly, they will inevitably come to blows. Just short of bloodshed the teacher will stop the scene, turn triumphantly to the class and point out, "You see, you must always play your action strongly."*

I used to teach that kind of improvisation myself. But after a time I was struck by a peculiar fact: all the scenes turn into melodrama. I have nothing against melodrama, but I wonder whether all of dramatic literature can be successfully acted in terms of what is essentially a melodramatic formula: one purpose coming into direct conflict with another.

I tried for years to do just that. I conscientiously analyzed every role I played or directed in terms of "action," "objective," and "super-objective." I found the process quite tortuous. Sometimes it seemed to me that there was no ulterior motive behind what a char-

---

*A notable exception to this kind of structuring is the "theater games" technique of improvisation pioneered by Viola Spolin and Paul Sills. Spolin and Sills were among the first to recognize the inadequacy of the action theory in improvisation.

acter did, no clear obstacle in his path, but I had been taught that there had to be, and so I considered myself stupid and kept looking. I got to be pretty good at thinking up infinitive phrases. For example, I once came to the conclusion that Macbeth's super-objective was "to destroy every threat to my ultimate security." That gave me a certain amount of intellectual satisfaction, but it somehow struck me as incongruous to think of Macbeth riding towards Forres at the opening of the play with that particular goal in mind. I found to my surprise that I could sometimes manage a scene quite well without reminding myself what I was after. At other times, when I tried to whip myself on towards a goal, I found that the words ceased to make sense, the behavior became illogical. I could "play my action" only by distorting what I intuitively felt to be there in the text.

All these difficulties vanished once I was able to give up the assumption that human beings are constantly absorbed in the pursuit of distant goals. Sometimes, of course, we do have a goal in mind, but sometimes we do not. We may walk in the woods for the purpose of getting someplace or for the immediate satisfaction of moving in pleasant surroundings.

Sometimes we are motivated partly by the distant prospect and partly by the immediate satisfaction. We want to get someplace and we want to do whatever it is that gets us there. But the more we really want to do something the less we have to bother ourselves about goals or rewards. When we are most alive it is the present doing, not the distant goal, that occupies us and absorbs our energies. As I type these words on this page, for example, I suppose I do have some goal in the back of my mind: "to persuade my readers to accept what I say," perhaps. I might even have a super-objective lurking about: "to be interviewed on the Dick Cavett Show as the world's foremost authority on acting." But as I write I do not feel that I am being pulled toward these goals. I do not envision some future bliss, dangled in front of my typewriter like a delectable carrot. I experience instead the present satisfaction of communicating, the fun of seeing the words fall into place, the thoughts becoming articulated on the page. I feel that I want to communicate something to you, and that seems to be mainly what makes me write.

Very often communication springs out of a wish to express something here and now, with no further purpose in mind. The communication is its own reward, for it relieves, at least temporarily, the psychic pressure that set it off. To find examples you need only open one of Chekhov's plays at random; you will probably discover a group of people who have come together for no earthshaking purpose (it may be just to pass a quiet afternoon on the lawn), and while they are there they are impelled to convey their regret for the lost possibilities of their lives, or their vision of the happiness of future generations, or their sense of ultimate redemption for an otherwise miserable and helpless mankind. There is no conflict in these scenes, but they are among the most dramatic ever written. They are full of life, because the people are filled with what they want to express.

Chekhov provides only the more obvious examples. Dramatic literature is full of situations in which the people seem more absorbed in what they want to express here and now than in the prospect of future gain. Romeo, standing beneath Juliet's balcony, is burning to convey what he feels about her. It is true that he will never rest till he holds her in his arms, and I have no objection if you want to call that an "action," but I cannot believe that he speaks <u>for the sake</u> of getting her, in the way that one might speak for the sake of getting ten dollars from a roommate. I cannot imagine him reminding himself, as he climbs over the wall, just what he's after, like a salesman thinking about his quota. I feel that he is driven on by something in him that needs to find words: Juliet is such an extraordinary creature that he has to improvise the most extravagant flights of language to come even close to conveying what he feels. It's all there in the text, Shakespeare articulated it, and the actor's job is to take it in and then let it come pouring out. But if the actor concentrates instead on trying to get something <u>from</u> Juliet, he is likely to look at her expectantly, his words will seem to serve some purpose beyond the immediate thing that wants to be conveyed, and the scene will look calculated, as if Romeo had it all worked out ahead of time.

The messenger at the end of <u>Oedipus the King</u> speaks of how Jocasta has just hung herself and Oedipus has jabbed out his eyes. Can we honestly say that he has set himself the purpose of trying to affect the crowd in some way, to achieve some result with them? Will he tell his story better if he reminds himself to "go after what I want"? When newscasters on television told of the assassination of John F. Kennedy, I doubt that they had to say to themselves before they went on, "All right, Walter, remember what you're trying to accomplish." Obviously they were deeply shaken, and those of us watching were moved to tears, but that was because the event itself, the thing they had to tell, was so overwhelming, the loss was so great and irremediable. If such messengers have a purpose, it is only to do their job: it falls to them to break the news. Perhaps they have to work to keep themselves under control rather than to urge themselves on. I sometimes wonder if they don't try first to get somebody else to go out and do it.

In <u>Waiting for Godot,</u> Didi and Gogo simply wait. And while they wait, they talk a good deal about their condition. But all the talk accomplishes nothing, except perhaps to pass the time. The point of the play is that there is nothing to be accomplished.

In many modern plays (Ionesco's are good examples), not only is there no goal to be pursued, there is no purpose in any sense to what people do. It is absolutely impossible to say why they do what they do. And it is not even important to ask. In these plays the actor has to act. His is not to reason why.

I readily admit that in some situations the character wants to get something from another person. But I emphatically deny that that is always the case. Very often what he wants is to communicate something to another person. If this were only a subtle theoretical distinction, it would hardly be worth troubling our heads over. But again and again I have seen actors run into deep trouble by persisting in the notion that they have to get something from somebody. The harder they try to find what they're "after," the further they move away from the true source of the scene: the pressure within the character that seeks to find release in words. They can fit the scene to the Procrustean bed of their theory only by mangling it.

Typically this mangling takes the form of speaking almost every line as if it expects a response from the other character. Here, for example, are a few lines of dialogue from the last scene of Lillian Hellman's The Children's Hour:

KAREN   ...Let's pack and get out of here. Let's take the train in the morning.

MARTHA The train to where?

KAREN   I don't know. Some place; any place.

MARTHA A job? Money?

KAREN   In a big place we could get something to do.

MARTHA They'd know about us. We've been famous.

KAREN   A small town, then.

MARTHA They'd know more about us.

KAREN   ...Isn't there anywhere to go?

MARTHA No. There'll never be any place for us to go. We're bad people. We'll sit. We'll be sitting the rest of our lives wondering what's happened to us. You think this scene is strange? Well, get used to it; we'll be here for a long time.

Start by asking what these two want from each other and only one answer is possible: Karen wants Martha to agree to go away, and Martha wants Karen to give up her plan. The scene is quickly locked into place. Inevitably the actresses will speak each line with the intention of convincing the other, and they will look after each line to see whether the other is convinced. The scene will become a kind of argument.

But start by asking what these two want to say to each other and an entirely different understanding of the text becomes possible. Here are two women whose lives have been wrecked by an accusation that they are lovers. Karen finds the prospect of staying on there intolerable. "Let's pack and get out of here," she says. "Let's take the train in the morning." That need not mean literally that she wants Martha to pack, it could simply be an expression of her longing to escape. (It would be very similar if, fed up with the academic life, I turned to a colleague and said, "Let's quit, let's turn in our resignations today and head for New York." He would know that I am not really trying to get him to go.) Martha says, "The train to where?" That doesn't have to be said as if she expects Karen to name a particular town; it could be an expression of regret that there is no place to go, a truth that is all too obvious. Karen replies, "I don't know. Some place; any place." I don't think she is pleading with Martha to go, I think she is saying that things are so hopeless here that it wouldn't matter where they went. Martha brings up the difficulties of getting accepted in a new place, and Karen seems to make light of these. But I don't see this as an argument. Karen, I think, is simply airing her opinion that things may not be as bad as they seem (an opinion that she does not hold very firmly herself). And Martha is commenting, with a kind of rueful humor, on the inevitability of their being stuck there forever. I have seen actresses play each line of this scene as if it seeks to elicit a sign of agreement from the other, as if the issue were whether they can really get away or not. (Both of them know very well that they can't, and they know the other knows.) I think they are driven not by a need to effect a change in each other but by a need to share their feelings about being trapped.

But what about scenes in which the character does try to get something from somebody? Is the action theory helpful here? I would say that it is precisely in such situations that the theory can be most misleading. For when we are after something from somebody we are seldom willing to acknowledge that we are and so we act as if we are not. Hedda Gabler, for example, wants to get Thea to spill the beans about her relationship with the man whom Hedda wants for herself. But she wants Thea to think that she is motivated by the concern and interest that would be expected from a close friend. "Now my darling little Thea," she says at one point, "I want you to tell me everything -- exactly as it is." I think that should be said no differently than if Thea were her best friend. But I have seen that moment (and indeed the whole scene) played with all the warmth and kindness of a cobra about to strike, and I have found it peculiar that Thea tells her exactly what she wants to know. The mistake, I suspect, is to play the "inner action" -- what Hedda hopes to gain from Thea -- rather than what Hedda wants to express to Thea.

Sometimes a character hides what he really wants, not in order to deceive anybody, but simply out of embarrassment or fear. A beautiful example occurs in the last act of The Cherry Orchard. Lopahin and Varya have been brought together so that he may propose to her, and they are both perfectly aware that that is why they are there. But she acts as if she came into the room to look for something, and he appears to be very interested in the weather. They don't do or say a single thing that would in any way lead to a proposal, and the scene ends with his running out of the room. How do you "play an action" when the character doesn't do anything about it? I don't think you can. Of course the actor and actress have to understand why they're there. But their purpose should never become manifest in anything they do, only perhaps in the difficulty they experience in keeping the conversation up. During the pauses each is probably searching for a way to broach the subject or waiting for the other to do so. At these moments it would be intolerable to look at each other. And yet I have often seen actors in this scene give each other long, significant stares, thus exposing themselves to the very danger that the characters cannot face. I think the stares are intended to tip off the audience to what the characters really want.

We always come back to the same point. Sometimes the character simply communicates what he feels (Romeo). Sometimes he communicates what he wants the other person to _think_ he feels (Hedda Gabler). And sometimes he cannot bear to communicate what he feels and so communicates something else, perhaps an opinion about the weather (Lopahin).

There may or may not be a distant goal in the character's mind, and if there is it is often hidden. True, there are some dramatic situations in which one character openly pursues an acknowledged goal: for instance, Oedipus tries to get Tiresias to tell him the truth revealed by the oracle, and Tiresias refuses. But here also the actor must discover exactly what Oedipus communicates in order to get Tiresias to give in.

In every case what the actor plays is what the character wishes to communicate.

Communicating is something that you can _do_. Wanting is not. I argued earlier that Stanislavsky never made a satisfactory distinction between wanting and doing. Several of his disciples have tried to make one, but I think they all go wrong by assuming that "doing" can only be physical. * For example, I.A. Rapoport points out that

_____

* Some of Stanislavsky's followers in America use the term "action"

knocking on a table is something you can do. He then argues that the doing will be different according to what you <u>want</u>: a) to test the firmness of the table or b) to quiet a group of people at a meeting. **

But Rapoport fails to see the essential difference between the two cases: knocking to test the firmness of the table is a simple physical act, complete in itself, but knocking in order to quiet the room is an act of communication that affects other people. And so in the second case there is a further question to be asked: What exactly do you want to convey by knocking? Given the purpose of quieting the room and the activity of knocking, you could still convey at least two very different things: (1) You feel that the people in the room ought to have quieted down long ago, and so you knock in a way that reprimands them for being unruly; or (2) you feel that they're having a fascinating conversation which they have every right to continue, and so you knock in a way that conveys regret at having to interrupt. In both cases you might achieve the same purpose: the room would quiet down. But the effect on the people would be quite different. They would clearly receive one of the two messages: that you blamed them or that you were sorry to interrupt. Obviously your message is conveyed not just by knocking, but with your whole face and body. You could even add words. You could say, "May I have your attention please" in a way that conveys either blame or regret.

Given any want, a human being can only <u>do</u> one of two things to satisfy it: (1) a simple physical act that leads directly to fulfillment or (2) an act of communication. This is evident in everyday life. Today, for example, I am beginning to feel oppressed by too many winter afternoons in the suburbs; my surroundings seem increasingly dull and monotonous. I begin to think of New York City, to picture myself walking down a street in Greenwich Village, dropping into a bookstore, perhaps seeing what's on at a favorite movie house. Very well, that is what I want, to get to the city. But what do I do about it? I might put on my coat, get into my car, and drive in, thus

---

to refer to what one wants and the term "activity" to refer to what one does. Others use the term "objective" to refer to what one wants and the term "action" to refer to what one does. When terminology is so confused one suspects an underlying confusion of thought. All the confusion is caused by the assumption that doing is essentially physical. When confronted with words, some teachers try to find physical equivalents: the actor "strokes" or "pierces" with words. But to me it makes more sense to admit that speech is what it is, communication, and to go about trying to pin down <u>what</u> is being communicated.

** "The Work of the Actor, " in <u>Acting: A Handbook of the Stanislavsky Method</u>, compiled by Toby Cole, New York, 1947, p. 51.

satisfying the need by direct physical activity. Or I might say to my wife, "I have a great idea: let's go into town to see a movie." I would then be expressing my delight at the prospect. Or I could say, "It's so boring around this house," expressing my feeling of discontent. Either of these communications might serve the purpose of getting her to agree to go. I might also work on her more directly, trying to convince her to overcome her reluctance: "Come on! Let's go!" But now suppose that circumstances prevent our going. I could still convey my feelings, not for the sake of getting anywhere, but simply to unburden myself. I might even go on at length, like one of Chekhov's three sisters, expressing my longing for the city and all it stands for.

Again we have come back to the same point. Whether the wish is to communicate something for its own sake or to get something, the doing can only be to communicate something -- unless of course the wish can be satisfied by direct physical action. But most dramatic situations require words. And it seems to me that the actor's search should be directed towards discovering what the character wishes to convey with the words.

The action theory demands a more complicated method of textual analysis. It assumes that the character's life is laid out in advance along neat lines, each purpose feeding into a larger one. It requires that the actor determine how the action in each "beat" (or small section of a scene) leads towards the objective of the whole scene and how the objective of the scene leads towards the super-objective of the play.

I cannot believe that human beings operate so methodically. Of course we have needs, but we tend to become absorbed by a present need until it is either satisfied or interrupted by a more pressing one, which forces its postponement. These needs are arranged linearly in time, not hierarchically by plan. We often do not know ourselves what we will want next. Sometimes we can satisfy a need by doing one act or speaking one word, and that need may then be replaced by a totally unexpected one. At other times we have to go on for quite a while before a need is satisfied.

If some overall need propels the character through large sections of the text, of course the actor must know what it is. In the next-to-last scene of Tennessee Williams' Summer and Smoke, Alma has learned that John is about to marry somebody else, and she rushes to his house, ready at last to give herself to him. Of course the actress must understand Alma's deep need for John and make it her own. But beyond this I part company with proponents of the action theory. I do not think the actress should work out an elaborate scheme of beats, actions, and objectives, all directed towards getting her man. (I cannot imagine Alma coming into the room with her head stuffed with all this.) I think the actress should just look closely at the text and try to grasp exactly what Alma communicates at each moment.

Alma probably doesn't know herself what she is going to do. She comes there because she has to, and when she gets there she doesn't know what to say, and so she stands there and waits for him to speak. When he doesn't, she says, "No greetings? No greetings at all?" She is expressing a somewhat playful surprise that he doesn't react to her sudden appearance after so long an absence.

At this point, and for some time afterwards, she communicates only what is safe. Of course we know why she's there, and John prob ably does too, simply from her arrival at this particular time. But both of them talk a good deal about sore throats and southern heating systems and a fox terrier that Alma used to have. Evidently it is intolerable for them to voice their deepest feelings -- intolerable for Alma because it is not easy to offer herself to a man, for John because it would be cruel for him to be the first to acknowledge why she is there.

And yet they cannot just stand there in silence, and so they talk about inconsequential things. All this while her need for him remains unconveyed. Alma finally takes a tentative step by suggesting that John listen to her heart through his stethescope. Even now it would not be too late for her to pull back and claim that she only wants to have her heart checked. But, "slowly, involuntarily, her hands lift and descend on the crown of his head... She bends down to a kneeling position in front of him and presses her mouth to his." She does this not out of some fixed resolve but almost, as Williams suggests, against her will. Nothing that she or John does is decided in advance. The scene could go any way at any moment. Alma could leave without letting John know how she feels. John could suddenly take her into his arms. Neither thing happens, but only because Williams chose to show us something else. Looking back we may say, yes, what he showed us makes a lot of sense, it's more or less what we would expect, knowing all that's happened between these two. But Alma and John are not trying to fulfill anybody's idea of how they ought to act. They are caught in the moment.

The action theory would require the actress to play the first half of the scene as if Alma does what she does in order to get John, as if her greeting him were only a necessary first step, before she can proceed to step two. But I think she does what she does because she cannot do anything else -- yet. I believe the actress has to stay with the moment. If she charges into the room hell-bent after John, she would be in great danger of passing over the first half of the scene in a rush. Or worse, she might try to express in the early part of the scene the very thing that Alma cannot bear to express, thus making nonsense of all the dialogue. But if the actress expresses only what is tolerable at the moment, the thing that is intolerable will lie there, waiting. Never fear that it will go away. The more the actress attends to other things, the more it will press forward, seeking release. When the moment comes, it will burst forth, out of control, as the expression of true passion always is.

What it comes down to is that you cannot convey two different messages at the same time. Of course the actor has to have a grasp of the whole situation, including those needs of the character that are not being attended to at the moment, but he can play only one thing at a time: what the character wishes to communicate here and now.

It may seem a bit silly to come back so often to such a simple point. But acting is simple, it's only the theories that are complicated. Talented people have always been able to do good work no matter what theories they subscribed to. Stanislavsky's own work, so far as I can gather, was not greatly impaired by any of the weaknesses I have pointed out in his theory. * He was too great a man to insist that his practice always follow his theory. There would be no need to point up the dangers implicit in the theory if his disciples, particularly in America, had not taken it so seriously.

I cannot resist making a brief detour to speculate on how this theory became so entrenched. It seems to have sprung out of the 19th-century psychology, with its fascination with "will." Perhaps in America it was fostered by the Puritan ethic, as if we would suddenly lapse into lassitude if we didn't continually remind ourselves to keep striving towards our Ulimate Reward, our Super-objective in the sky. Finally, the idea may have been nourished by our commercial thinking: before doing anything we are conditioned to ask, "What's in it for me?"

No matter why actors cling to the theory, I can see several advantages to letting go of it. First, a whole new range of situations become accessible: those in which the character is motivated not by a distant goal but by a pressure within him that seeks to find release in words.

Second, the actor will find it easier to play people different from himself. If he asks only, "What would I want if I were in these circumstances?" he might want something quite different from what the character wants, or even if he happens to want the same thing, he might do something very different about it. An experienced actress, asked what she would do if she were in St. Joan's situation, replied, very much to the point, "I'd stay home and mind the sheep." But if she were asked instead, "What is Joan doing here?" the answer would lie right there in the text. If she can just do it, she will begin to act in a way that might astonish those who know here only in her everyday life.

Abandoning the action theory also frees the actor from the obligation of forcing every line to fit a preconceived pattern. I have often heard actors ask, "What's my action?" as if a single infinitive from the coach would solve all their problems. Once handed their infinitive they dash down the field with it, squashing out all differences, trampling on every inconsistency, obliterating all subtlety in their headlong pursuit of what they want. An opposite problem comes up when the conscientious actor tries to divide each scene into "beats." Some scenes appear

---

* See my article, "The Stanislavsky System in Russia," The Drama Review, March, 1973.

to be one long "beat," in the sense that the character communicates the same thing over and over in different words. And there are other scenes in which the character communicates something different in every line.

Actors tend to cling to an action because it protects them from being unsure of where they're going. It's a kind of magic key. Knowing and rehearsing the doings ahead of time will also give an actor security. But in another sense, the actor ought not to be protected from uncertainty. He ought to step on stage with no more knowledge of how things will work out than the character possesses. Reminding himself of his purpose ("Remember what you're after now") will make it difficult for him to attend to what actually happens. But if he just comes in and attends to the first thing, then a fresh impulse will arrive, and he will attend to that, and then another, and so on. True, that way is more dangerous. But actors have to take their chances, just like people.

Directors tend to use the action approach as a way of whipping actors on, as if they were all sluggards at heart. "Go, go, go" they are told, "Get what you want! Try harder!" I suspect what they really mean is, "For Christ's sake, don't bore your audience," because in America that is the one unpardonable sin. But audiences can be just as bored by frenetic, meaningless activity as they can by inactivity. The question is not whether we want a lot of activity or not. The question is what kind of life ought to be present here, and how can we live that life fully and spontaneously, whether it be a moment of quiet joy or a cry of anguish. Life takes many forms, and it is never boring to one who loves it all.

I believe the actor must throw away the whip. Not just the whip of the action theory, but all the other whips, all the admonitions that teachers and directors keep urging on him, and that he urges on himself if they aren't around to do it for him. For I think that if he could just sit back quietly for a minute and subtract all the things that he does not have to do, the one thing that he does have to do will stand out so clearly that nobody could possibly miss it. As Sherlock Holmes remarked to Dr. Watson, "When you have excluded the impossible, whatever remains, however improbable, must be the truth." I think that applies to acting in the sense that the way to act a given moment is improbably simple and inevitably right. Like Dr. Watson, we should have seen it all along but we didn't.

What gets in the actor's way nine times out of ten is trying to adhere to some formula that really doesn't make any sense. Actually, much of what Stanislavsky said about acting makes very good sense indeed. He illuminated acting for us in as startling a way as Freud illuminated the psyche. If we can take his insights and keep working on them we can continue to grow as he did. But if we take what he said as a rigid, unchangeable formula, we are likely to bottle ourselves up. We tend to do that in America because we in the theatre are afraid --

36

we don't get to work enough, that's the trouble -- and we look for a teaching that will save us. But the actor who is no longer afraid doesn't need to be saved. If he can free himself of all obligation to do what he needn't do, he can begin to understand the one thing he must do: what the character does at the moment.

"IF ONLY I COULD BE AS EXPRESSIVE AS MY DREAMS"
An Account of the First Phase of Work
at Stage Two in London

JAMES ROOSE-EVANS

>True creative excitement, which demands
the inward image to be expressed in some
outward form, depends, it would seem, on
a deeper kind of stimulation, on the exis-
tence of an idea, however vague, the deter-
mination to give it expression, and the sen-
sibility and experience to find for it appropriate form.

>John Allen

(The following excerpt is from the author's Experimental Theatre,
second edition, published by Universe Books, New York. It describes
the work of Stage Two and provides a valuable introduction to the
author's present piece. Ed.)

>It is only now that the drama has begun to be aware of
the potency of sound. Ted Hughes argues that there
exists in the human race a common tonal consciousness, "a language belonging below the levels where
differences appear." Similarly Jung maintained that
we all share, at a deeper level, a "collective unconscious."

Of course the actor has first to get at the emotion, or tap those
archetypes that lie dormant in the collective unconscious. It is toward
this end that the long discipline is directed, in the work of Peter Brook's
Centre, of the Roy Hart Theatre, and of Grotowski's Laboratory Theatre.

Working on such a level means that one visual image, or one word, can therefore often prove more expressive than a whole speech.

In Stages, the first work created by Stage Two, there is a sequence in which the actor, Hywel Jones, speaks only one word. The word, a meditation on death, is set among several coffins placed like tombs. On one of these Hywel Jones lies, bound from head to foot in a winding shroud. From within the tombs are heard the voices of the dead calling out to each other, using their own names: Paul, Di, Kevin, Hywel. Hearing his own name called, the shrouded figure stirs, is awakened, as it were, from centuries of sleep. During the rehearsal period I came across these words from Jung's Seven Sermons to the Dead, which seemed to me to express much of what we were seeking: "The dead came back from Jerusalem where they found not what they sought ... in the night the dead stood along the wall and cried 'We would have knowledge of God. Where is God? Is God dead?' Now the dead howled for they were unperfected."

The shrouded figure struggles to break out of his bonds; he falls off the tomb and rolls forward on the ground. The sense of struggle inside the shroud is very intense, almost as though the actor were so tightly bound that he may not be able to get out. He cries out in his terror and we hear his breathing, as though he were fighting his way up through the earth. Finally he breaks through the material, sweat streaming down his face, the eyeballs dilated in terror. He gazes upward intently, murmuring frantically the sound, "Li-li-li-li!"

Then, as he fully realizes his release from the claustrophobic bonds of the grave, as he comprehends the sense of space, of freedom, of light, the sound becomes the word "Li-Light!" Suddenly he turns to the other coffins, throwing off the lid of each in turn, now crying out the word "Light! Light! Light!" like a trumpet summoning the dead to the day of resurrection.

Into that one sound the actor pours all the intensity of a life experience. The image is personal to the actor yet re-created for each performance. The vibrations of that one word, charged with the actor's deep emotion, convey to us who hear, the experience of darkness, which is the opposite to light, the fear of being buried alive which is part of the taboo of death, as well as the awe and terror of being saved, of being delivered up to a new life. In this sequence the actor had earned his right to say the one word, "Light."

The search today is for "a necessary theatre, one which is an urgent presence in our lives, speaking as Artaud envisioned, to its audience at a depth of feeling that precedes the dissection of man into social and psychological categories, speaking to a man in his wholeness." (Peter Brook)

INTRODUCTION TO THE EXERCISES

Many of these exercises were first evolved when I was teaching at the Juilliard School of Music in New York from 1955-6. Others grew out of the first Stage Two Workshop period. The only actual Grotowski exercises used are those relating to the vocal resonators.

There is no mystique about these exercises but they are difficult and should be taught only by someone who has experienced the work and so made his own discoveries. They cannot be taught by rote or at random outside of an integrated system of training. I say this because one sees all too often, especially in America, theatre departmemts at colleges and universities claiming to teach the techniques of Stanislavsky, Brecht, Grotowski, Nikolais, Graham, Open Theater etc. all within the space of one or two years. One ought also to add here a word of warning. The fashionable popularity of Encounter groups (the Esalen techniques) as well as the hypnotic attraction of psychic contents for the psychologically maladjusted and immature, have resulted in scores of teachers in colleges dabbling with the psychic contents of their 19-20-year-old students. In the hands of an inexperienced and immature teacher, one who has little self-knowledge, this can be very dangerous. As to Grotowski's techniques, it must be remembered that they are intended for highly-trained professional actors who, as mature adults, are totally committed to a particular way of work and kind of theatre. Grotowski himself, and rightly, disclaims many of those who claim to be his disciples.

Among the exercises that follow there are a number that I would not use with young people and certainly not in any preliminary sessions. The teacher is responsible for whatever psychic contents he releases in the student and he may well find himself, like Pandora, totally unequipped to deal with a particular situation. Only in the presence of an experienced teacher, and among a group of individuals who respect and trust each other, can certain exercises such as Frontier or Shroud be attempted.

While the exercises are in progress there should be no interruption and no talking, no audible reaction, whether of laughter or boredom. The exercises are not performances; they do not seek to entertain but to make discoveries. They are a part of the continuing process of research into the actor's craft. Those watching have to exercise a disciplined watchfulness that transcends boredom, fatigue or superficial amusement. The actor watching is as totally involved as the actor carrying out the exercise. Therefore the actor who is watching never slouches but uses the very act of sitting as an exercise in itself. He sits upright, with erect spine, breathing regularly, his concentration fixed upon the exercise in front of him. If he has knowledge of the Mathias Alexander Technique he will apply this while sitting in this position.

In the exercises that follow the actor is confronted with an image to which he has to give a total response. However, he responds not mimetically (his concern is not to tell a story) but spontaneously, as might a child. Therefore the response of each actor, each person,

41

will be different. The actor cannot know in advance what he will do, and during the exercise he must not intellectualize or start "acting." What is "acting"? By this I mean naturalistic acting in which the emphasis is primarily upon the thought processes of the "character." Give the average actor an improvisation and he will move mainly in an upright position, physically very tense and inexpressive, but a great deal is going on in the eyes, in the head.

Our exercises seek a physical and emotional response and are noncerebral. It is through action that the actor expresses himself. This is nothing new; it is what Stanislavsky was always saying. But in these exercises it is not naturalistic action that is the aim, but a free, spontaneous and imaginative response of the body that would be natural in a child or in a dancer of the Modern Dance school. Yet at the same time the actor's intelligence provides the reins of control so that while freely following his intuitive response to the image given, he has control of his musculature, breathing and vocal equipment. Therefore the actor is never in danger of hurting himself or others, even in a very vigorous or seemingly violent improvisation. It is rather like Zen in that the actor is being acted upon by something deeper in his nature; he is an instrument being willingly played upon.

In our work we are trying to tap the depths of each person, the unconscious, and to give form to his aspirations, intimations and intuitions -- feelings which in most people are not even acknowledged or recognized but which, once realized and given form, can add meaning and depth to the life of the community. This is why in our work we devote so much time and energy and discipline to acquiring technical skills.

In The Cult of Sincerity Sir Herbert Read says:

> Art is an instrument for tilling the human psyche that
> it may continue to yield a harvest of rich beauty ...
> art is the definition, the delimitation, of feeling ...
> a work of art is a feeling in-formed.

> ... Since each individual is unique, his feelings will
> be peculiar to himself, and he must find the exact
> words to express this peculiarity. He is sincere in
> the degree of the exactitude of this equation. Feeling
> comes in aid of feeling, as Wordsworth said; the feel-
> ing for the value of the words helps to define the feel-
> ing itself. That is what I mean by sincerity, but I do
> not wish to disguise the difficulty, and the rarity, of
> the process.

The common failure, he observes, is to allow habitual words and phrases -- and in our work gestures, movements, sounds -- flowing spontaneously from the memory to determine and deform the feeling. "The whole exercise," he concludes, "is one of exquisite perception and instinctive judgment."

The actor will not arrive at the following exercises easily and he will often despair. He has to learn to give up looking for results or attempting to manipulate or program the results. He has to sit loosely to the exercise and allow it to take over. When the exercise has come to its inevitable conclusion, and with practice he will learn to recognize when this has happened, he will reflect upon the content of what he has just done, as well as recall in his mind's eye its outward form. He then should be able to repeat the exercise with the added awareness of what he is trying to communicate.

Every work has its own innate length, rhythm, spacing, dynamics, and these exercises will develop in the actor a heightened awareness of the organic laws of creation.

The exercises must begin with a period of concentration until all outside distractions are removed and the actor is aware only of himself and the object-image with which he is confronted. If necessary it may be five minutes before he moves. Yet he must not become quietist or passive else he will lose the impetus to act. Once he has an impetus to move he must go with that first movement and discover where it leads him. He is himself both involved and not involved, he is the watcher and the doer. If I stress the importance of concentration it is because it is often all too easy just to play. Such peripheral activity will lead nowhere and will go on indefinitely until the individual is either exhausted or bored.

Because so much confusion and vagueness and general emoting exist under the name of improvisation, especially in the educational field, it is important to stress the role of consciousness. If the unconscious, once in action, is left to itself, there is a risk that its contents will become over-powering, or will manifest their negative, destructive side. Left to itself it can destroy its own gifts and sooner or later sweep them into annihilation. But as Carl Jung has shown, it is consciousness that holds the key to the values of the unconscious, and that therefore plays a decisive part.

> Consciousness alone is competent to determine the
> meaning of the images and to recognize their signif-
> icance for man here and now, in the concrete reality
> of the present. Only in an interplay of consciousness
> and the unconscious can the unconscious prove its
> value, and perhaps even show a way to overcome the
> melancholy of the void.
>
> (Aniela Jaffe, "Symbolism in the Visual
> Arts," published in Man and His
> Symbols: Aldus Books)

When the actor is working with materials, he has to learn how to respond to their innate qualities, whether they be of wood, stone, bamboo, silk, canvas etc. He has to learn how to work with the material. He must not impose his ego upon it, demonstrating his cleverness, or use it naturalistically -- perhaps by way of adornment -- but allow the material to draw forth some response from within himself. It is for the actor to discover the essence of bamboo, of silk, of unwieldy poles. In this way the material will come to be an extension of the actor himself. We who are watching shall not be conscious of the actor being clever with his props, but we shall be aware of a total shape and pattern, of actor and material working together.

In a significant survey, Drama in Education, written for the Department of Education and Science, John Allen has some profound comments on dramatic play that are very pertinent to our way of working. He refers to Professor Huizinga's observation that an element of play lies at the heart of a great deal of our art and culture. John Allen then continues: "When we play with an object or material we discover something about its nature. We are, in a sense, investigating its essence. Our faculties are usually relaxed and aspects of whatever it is we are playing with become apparent by accident and unintentionally. There may develop a sense of direction or purpose in our play so that we become inventive and creative. The curious and important corollary of this is that at the same time we appear to learn something about our own identity."

Speaking of the way children go into a play corner and act out a scene, he remarks how "they are giving expression to some idea that demands expression." So, too, in our work. So in all art. But for the actor this experience is less common because, in general, he is called upon to be an interpreter and not an original creative artist. In our work the actor is handed no text, no scenario, not even the given circumstances of a Stanislavsky improvisation. He starts in a void with nothing. Quite literally, he creates something out of nothing.

In silent concentration he waits for a first movement or sound. He then goes with that sound or movement and follows it like a thread. Perhaps the process is most clearly expressed by the abstract painter Jackson Pollock, who revealed that he painted in a kind of trance: "When I am in my painting I am not aware of what I am doing. It is only after a sort of 'get acquainted' period that I see what I have been about. I have no fears about making changes, destroying the image, etc. because the painting has a life of its own. I try to let it come through. It is only whan I lose contact with the painting that the result is a mess. Otherwise there is pure harmony, an easy give and take, and the painting comes out well."

The painter, the sculptor, the composer, the writer, works alone. The process, arduous enough, becomes more demanding when a group of actors is involved, since in any group improvisation no actor can follow his own impulse at the expense of the others. Gradually, however, there develops a group telepathy, an instinctive awareness of one another, an immediate give and take.

All this is difficult to put into words and I always urge someone who is new to the work to try the exercise with as little explanation on my part as is possible. It is only by doing that he can learn, by his own experience rather than by my words. And every time the exercise goes astray he will have learned something more.

Two or three years ago Barbara Hepworth recommended to me a small book called Zen in the Art of Archery. The book is by a German philosopher, Eugen Herrigel, who studied under a Zen Master in Japan for seven years. It is a book I have read and re-read and keep by me always. Subsequently I learned from Martin Esslin that when he met Jerzy Grotowski in Wroclaw, Grotowski revealed to him that it was this small book that had influenced him more than anything else. The following passage describes exactly the way in which to approach the exercises that follow:

"The right art" cried the Master, "is purposeless, aimless! The more obstinately you try to learn how to shoot the arrow for the sake of hitting the goal, the less you will succeed in the one and the further the other will recede. What stands in your way is that you have a much too wilful will. You think that what you do not do yourself does not happen."

"But you yourself have told me often enough that archery is not a pastime, not a purposeless game, but a matter of life and death!"

"I stand by that. We master archers say: one shot -- one life! What this means you cannot yet understand..."

"What must I do then?" I asked thoughtfully.

"You must learn to wait properly."

"And how does one learn that?"

"By letting go of yourself and everything yours behind you so decisively that nothing more is left of you but a purposeless tension."

"So I must become purposeless -- on purpose?" I heard myself say.

"No pupil has ever asked me that, so I don't know the right answer."

"And when do we begin these new exercises?"

"Wait until it is time."

"A true game is one that frees the spirit ...
   the true game, as Locke recognized years ago,
   is the one that arises from the players themselves."

   from the introduction to
   Children's Games In Streets And
   Playgrounds by Iona and Peter Opie

THE FIRST EXERCISES

The hand exercise

This consists of kneeling on the floor and concentrating on the hands which are placed palm down on the floor in front of one. Eventually one or both hands will make a movement which will then set in motion a whole sequence of movements. The actor has to go with the exercise, and be prepared to see where his hands will lead him, as though they were trying to communicate something to him -- as indeed they often are. It is not a question of making pretty and aesthetic movements. The exercise should never be movement for its own sake.

The actor is allowing a statement to be made through his whole body but concentrated in the movement of the hands. He is an instrument through which a mood, a conflict, an emotion, part of himself, is being expressed. With practice he will know when the improvisation has come to an end and often it is only at the end, as he thinks back, that he will realize what has happened. If the exercise contains a germinal image, the actor will explore it in further improvisations, refining it, until it becomes a finished work ready for performance.

The exercise had its genesis in a dance work which I saw in New York in 1955 performed by the modern dancer, Sybil Shearer. The dance was called, Seven Images of an Answer. The first Image commenced with the dancer seated on the floor and only the hands moving, reaching out from side to side, above and below, in a pondering search, as though probing the space immediately round the body. Slowly the dancer rose, the hands mounting one above the other, reaching high up, cutting and slicing space. Suddenly the hands dropped, falling away, as though chasms were opening and abysses of darkness had been revealed.

The work ended with the dancer once again seated, cross-legged, and now for the first time the hands came together, palm to palm, as though in prayer lay the answer. I was reminded of Wordsworth's:

   Those obstinate questionings
   Of sense and outward things,
   Fallings from us, vanishings,
   Blank misgivings of a creature
   Moving about in worlds not realized,

46

High instincts before which our mortal nature
Did tremble like a guilty thing surprised.

The hand exercise for two

Two actors face each other, on their knees, palms on the ground. They relate to each other through the hands. They never look each other in the face, in the eye, but concentrate upon the two pairs of hands, albeit aware of the rest of the body. The exercise is a conversation of hands. Between two people who have never even met before it is possible to set up strong vibrations, so that a true communion takes place between them.

Ritual of hands

A group of not more than six kneel in a tight circle, hands on the floor, all kneeling, facing inwards. In each of these exercises the actors must remain on their knees, but within that limitation there is much space to be discovered and used. The early stages of this exercise, the first few improvisations, nearly always reveal conflict and aggression, different individuals trying to assert themselves. Once this stage is passed then this exercise will take off of its own accord.

The frontier exercise

A long pole or length of sticky tape on the floor denotes the frontier. The actor is stationed at the other end of the studio. He sets out, from any starting position he chooses, on an imaginary, dreamlike journey to a frontier.

What is the frontier? What is at the frontier? Will he cross it? Does he want to? And if he does, what is on the other side and is it what he expected? For everyone the exercise is different, and so long as the individual responds directly to the image, avoiding narrative or mime, it is psychologically revealing and can tell the observant actors much about the temperament and inner life of each other, the hidden conflicts and fantasies. Naturally, working in this very vulnerable way presupposes no outside observers, as well as an absolute trust between the actors and their director.

With all these exercises, where the director senses that some discussion would be helpful, this should be encouraged. With this particular exercise the actor will begin to consider the many different kinds of frontiers that exist, between neighbor and neighbor, race and race, North and South, Dr. Jekyll and Mr. Hyde. Someone will recall Robert Frost's poem on Mending Wall; another the frontier of some personal decision, the threshold of life, the crossing from innocence to experience; the need to declare one's identity and show one's passport; the yearning for some Utopia, some Eldorado, some Lost Horizon; the fear of the Unknown. One will instance the frontier of the mirror, how Alice goes through the Looking-Glass, and in Cocteau's film of Orphee, how Death leads Orphee through the looking-glass into the underworld; the frontier of the River Styx, the boundaries of Heaven and Hell, the boundaries between parent and child, and the initiation ceremonies of certain tribes when the youth is thrust out into the wilderness, the jungle, and so crosses the frontier into manhood. And so on.

The frontier exercise has various permutations as a group exercise. What happens when one person approaches the frontier from one side, and a small group approaches from the other? Or one group from one side and another group from the other side? What happens when they meet? What happens if one group approaches the frontier?

The rope exercise
As a solo exercise: the actor has a length of rope that is looped at either end around his big toes. The rope should be long enough so that when he stretches his arms in the air he just stretches the rope taut. The rope is part of him, as though he had been born with it, his shadow, something he cannot escape and must learn to live with. Technically he must always keep the rope taut, never letting it fall slack. He must be keenly aware of the shapes he is cutting in space, sense the images evolving.

As an exercise for two people:
For this a longer length of rope is required, about thirty feet. This is knotted so as to form a circle. One actor sits on a chair holding two lengths, one in each hand, as though holding the reins. The other actor stands as far away as the rope will permit with part of it looped about his waist. He can move but the other actor must stay seated on the chair. Each controls the rope with his hands. The aim is to develop a relationship through the spatial lines and patterns created by control of the rope, thereby setting up a dramatic/emotional situation.

As a group exercise:
Three, or not more than five, actors take hold of the rope. They always maintain hold of the rope, letting it slide through their hands when necessary. The important thing is to keep the rope taut. If it becomes slack it will merely get entangled and knotted. However complex the patterns created in space the actors must be able to unravel them swiftly.

The shroud exercise
About thirty feet of butter muslin is required. One end is placed over the actor's head, reaching down to his ankles. The rest is then wound round him from his head downwards, and finally is knotted off at his ankles. While the actor is being bound up he must keep his arms at his sides. His feet are left free. He is laid on the ground.

He lies there for as long as he wants. He absorbs the experience of being tightly bound, imagining himself lying under the ground, perhaps for centuries. He must commence when he feels himself moved, compelled, and it is through action that he will give expression to his emotional response. There is no value in the actor merely lying inside the shroud thinking/feeling because this will not communicate to us. Expression must occur through action.

This can be a very frightening exercise for certain people, and outside of a professional group of actors, should not be given to anyone who is emotionally unstable. Because such exercises touch a very deep level in the individual, the actor should be encouraged to feel that he has all the time he wants. He must never be made to feel that he is being rushed, that he is boring the others. There is no deadline.

Of course, when an actor is working on a piece for performance then he does have to think of time.

In our work we do not improvise in a performance. Every detail is refined in rehearsal until the work is ready to be·shared with an audience.

What is dramatic time? There are no rules. An actor without talent has no instinctive sense of dramatic timing; a talented actor does. Dramatic time is as long as the talented actor's dramatic sense tells him it is, or as he is guided by his director. A pause is its own length. The Living Theatre demonstrated that a pause may be longer than we ever dreamed it could be. So, too, with the Bread and Puppet Theatre. Sometimes, with such groups, we are made to wait so long that we have gone beyond the point of fatigue. Our defenses are down and we are vulnerable to the image. What is of importance is the image itself. If it is merely trivial then we are frustrated, wounded.

The figure on the white cloth exercise

A piece of white cloth, twelve feet by twelve feet, is stretched on the floor. One actor lies in the center, on or under the material. Four actors, one to each corner, keep vigil. They respond to the image of the person in the center as a corpse.

Another white cloth exercise, for two people

The two actors stand facing each other, holding the material on the level of their chins, the material stretched taut between them. It is as though they are standing at a high table. They must, as in the above exercise, control the cloth with their hands, carving shapes with it. They must not use it naturalistically. There are many variations with these exercises and with different materials and different colors.

The wooden poles exercise

About a dozen wooden poles, six feet in length and of a width that the actor can grip in his hand. Any starting point the actor chooses.

In our work, Jarkko Tamminen entered with one pole across his neck, his arms looped over it, and his eyes closed, like the blind Oedipus. As he traversed his feet touched pole after pole on the floor. Gradually he gathered all these poles. He struggled to hold all of them in his arms, the poles sliding and slipping. He was like a man with many problems. Then, swiftly, with a determined effort, he seized them in a bundle and in excitement raced round the hall, his eyes suddenly opened. But he lost control of them and they slithered to the floor. He fell, slowly reached out for one pole, realizing that he must cope with one problem at a time. Jarkko Tamminen's use of the poles called to mind the poen The Armful by Robert Frost:

For every parcel I stoop down to seize,
I lose some other off my arms and knees,
And the whole pile is slipping, bottles, buns,
Extremes too hard to comprehend at once,
Yet nothing I should care to leave behind.
With all I have to hold with, hand and mind,
And heart if need be, I will do my best
To keep their building balanced at my breast.
I crouch down to prevent them as they fall;
Then sit down in the middle of them all.
I had to drop the armful in the road
And try to stack them in a better load.

This image, discovered in an improvisation, was subsequently used in the production of Oedipus.

Exercises with space

The actor will attach a length of rope or a length of elastic to a place high up on a wall. A group of actors, each attached to a different spot. Explore.

Build a series of levels. Give each actor a large bamboo frame and let him explore the levels of space as well as the manipulation in space, on these different levels, with these frames.

Wood, bamboo, silk, cloth, newspaper, candles, ropes, ladders, chairs, boxes, tubes, bags, sacks, tables, tree trunks, masks, swings -- almost anything can be used to stimulate the imagination of the actor. And as he works with these materials so he learns their various properties. He discovers that he can create out of almost anything. Gradually he builds up an armory of images, like a poet his vocabulary. He amasses, like a craftsman, a ground of experience. There is much waste and many mistakes. He learns to discard, to throw away.

I recall Barbara Hepworth saying, "We must go on creating else the world, and the Philistines, will close in." She referred to the courage one needs to throw away, if need be, when one is creating.

"Once a work is lost you mustn't try to hang on to it. Let it go. The courage to smash." She paused and smiled. "I smash less now because I am more mature. But we have to risk failures and be prepared to start all over again. We have to follow the thread. Most of us have only one thread but we must hang on to it. . . . You have to be open to the work. Sometimes when I get stuck, I go to sleep for twenty minutes, and then when I wake up, the problem is resolved.

"We have to risk failures and be prepared to start all over again." That is what this work is about.

THE FIRST VOCAL EXERCISES

All vocal classes should begin with breathing exercises. In due course the actor will evolve his own set of exercises but the simple one that I use is as follows.

Lie flat on your back and listen to your breathing, to the beating of your heart. Then raise your right arm in a sweeping gesture and bring the hand close to your face. Close your right nostril with your right thumb (keeping the other fingers relaxed and outspread) and breathe in vigorously through your left nostril counting up to three mentally as you inhale. Then shut your left nostril with the ring finger (both nostrils are now closed) and hold your breath, counting up to twelve without any hurry. Keeping your left nostril shut, release your right and breathe out, counting up to six. Then breathe in again through the same nostril, counting up to three; close it and hold your breath for a count of twelve; release your left nostril and breathe out on six. This constitutes one complete cycle, what is called a pranayama. Continue for five cycles, always beginning and ending with your left nostril.

These exercises must be done slowly and rhythmically, breathing in and breathing out, like the coming in and going out of the tide, advancing and receding. Some teachers recommend keeping your eyes closed. I prefer to keep them open so that the actor maintains an awareness of the space around him, in addition to guarding against dozing off.

Once familiarized the student can make simple experiments. For instance, during the first inhalation he can concentrate on filling the base of his left lung; he then imagines the air filling out the left side, and during the holding in of the breath (what is called the apnoe) he can let the air spread all through his left lung. Then the other lung. Then both lungs.

These exercises have a deeply calming effect, enabling the individual to concentrate more steadily. As Pere Dechanet states in his book, A Christian Yoga: "To breathe calmly and steadily is also to think. So if you find yourself compelled to deal with some important matter or to take some decision, or face some difficulty, do not hesitate to carry out some pranayamas first."

The Resonators

The explanation of these is set out in Grotowski's book, Towards a Poor Theatre. The actor must learn to do his own research with the director watching each actor in turn. The exercises cannot be done in a class. They necessitate each actor being in a separate room.

The exercises call for complete concentration, of mind, body and voice. As Grotowski makes plain they must not be treated as vocal exercises separate from movement or motivation. The actor is not trying to achieve particular sounds like a singer practicing his scales. Everything must be motivated and given an emotional association by the actor himself.

For instance, if working on the head resonators, the actor might choose one morning to concentrate on the resonator at the top of the skull, that at the back, and that in the front. Standing in the middle of the studio he may take the sound -- King! and repeat it swiftly for 10 to 15 minutes. As he stands there his imagination might suggest wild geese flying overhead, almost as though he were calling them. Commence with the resonator in the front of the skull and imagine them flying towards him; then as they fly directly overhead, change to the resonator at the top of the skull. Finally, as they fly away and recede into the distance behind him, move to the resonator at the back of the skull. He may then try to vary this with volume to suggest their approach and retreat. At the same time he will be reacting emotionally to the thought of the geese, while the geese themselves may become a symbol of something else desired.

There is absolutely no value to doing these exercises perfunctorily for a few minutes. They must be carried out with total concentration. If the actor tires he must incorporate his tiredness into the exercise, into the quality of sound he is creating.

Just as he does with Grotowski's exercise, Plastique, the actor learns to create his own variations with the use of the resonators. Each day the actor must go through all the resonators in turn. He may begin with legs astride, gripping the ground firmly with his feet, and flopping down, arms dangling (but without squashing the diaphragm). From this position, or even on all fours, he will commence with the stomach resonator. He will feel the weight of his body, the sense of the ground beneath him, its depths, the heaviness of soil, and begin to direct the sound from the resonator in his stomach. It is as though through his stomach he were trying to communicate with the center of the earth. According to his mood that day, various emotions will color the exercise. If he is feeling sad then through the sound he may express shades of grief, of lamentation, of loss. Crawling about the floor he may break into keening, as though seeking in the depths of the earth or among the ruins of some destroyed city for those that are lost. The deepest sound, the bass, comes from the stomach, and at times the actor will have the sensation of boring into the ground, plumbing its depths, sinking deeper and deeper.

The exercises must be done in private or with the director or a fellow actor present. The actor must hold nothing back but learn to freely express a whole variety of emotions through the use of sound and yet always he must check that he is using the correct resonator and that his voice has not slipped back to the throat.

In his own time, he will move next to the chest resonator and so on, in sequence. And his bodily movement will reflect this progress, so that by the time he is reaching the highest sound, through the use of the resonator in the top of the head, he may well be walking on air. With this resonator he may start a furious or comic argument with the ceiling or God or some imagined being up there, or identify with a poised and trilling lark, or a hovering and swooping hawk.

The entire sequence, when properly carried out, will not only have fully flexed the voice and the breathing apparatus but will have stretched the actor imaginatively and emotionally, further coordinating movement, voice and inner emotion. When the actor is using the whole of himself correctly he will not be tired but will draw fresh energy from these exercises. If he feels that he is straining then he should pause and for a few minutes carry out breathing exercises.

The Icarus exercise

At some point I suggested to my actors that they should explore certain myths through sound and movement, but predominantly in sound. Icarus was the young man who wanted to fly and so his father Daedalus made for him wings out of wax and feathers. But Icarus, in his confidence, flew too near the sun, the wax melted and he plummeted to his death.

The aim of the exercise is not to tell this story by way of illustration. The actor needs to reflect on the image for some days, identifying with it personally. He is Icarus, Icarus is himself. In attempting the exercise it must become an identification with the Icarus within the actor, his own aspirations, ambitions, his own attempts to transcend himself, to take flight, escape even. To repeat Grotowski: "One must give totally in one's deepest intimacy, with confidence, as when one gives oneself in love."

If the actor does this then the exercise, as with all the work, will be different and unique to each actor. A company of actors performing the Icarus exercise would each create an individual and personal rendering of the myth. It would, in fact, then become his personal myth -- just as in dreams archetypal figures take on different associations, according to the individual dreamer.

The Leda exercise

Where Icarus is particularly suited as an image for men, that of Leda is intended for women. The god Jove so desired Leda that he turned himself into a swan and raped her.

The closed box exercise

Pandora was so curious to know what was inside the locked box, which she had been instructed not to open, that she did open it and so let out all the evils into the world.

Again, the identification must be personal. What is it within myself that I want to open, what unresolved problem? It may be that I have no desire to open the box (this will depend upon the psychological maturity of the individual actor), or that the box represents something sacred and numinous and thereby becomes the unveiling of a tabernacle, a source of Mana, of spiritual energy. All this the actor explores vocally, in abstract sound, employing the resonators, with a minimum of movement.

It is important for the actor to use the resonators consciously.

Texts

The actor takes a short poem, such as John Donne's sonnet on death. He says the poem over and over, each time discovering new colorings, new meanings, new inflections, new associations. As he does so certain key words, phrases or images may tug at him. He will then freely associate with that particular image. He might take the word 'death' and break it up into its different sounds -- 'd', 'ea', and 'th'. He will use these sounds to explore his own spontaneous reaction to the image of death. The word/sound acts as a springboard, a point of departure. Eventually he will return to the word 'death' and continue with the sonnet. En route he may discover other key words. After many improvisations he will have gathered two or three that move him particularly, that serve to deepen his understanding of the poem as well as of himself.

The name exercise

The actor takes his own name and uses the sound to explore his own identity. At the end when the actor says, quite simply:

I am Hywel

I am Kevin

I am Diana

I am Paul

we who are watching have a deeper awareness of the identity of that person.

THE PHYSICAL EXERCISES

The aim is to develop the actor's physical expressiveness so that his body will respond to the demands of his imagination, to the fullest extent of his particular physique and talent. Although the actor is expected to have the mobility and plasticity of the dancer he is not being trained to be a dancer, and therefore it is important to avoid imposing upon him any strongly differentiated style of movement, whether it be that of ballet or modern dance. What is aimed at is a physical discipline, resilience, and expressiveness that are not normally required of an actor. Given such a thorough base he is then able to work on his own, and develop such further skills as may be required by the work he is doing. In our work the actor does three hours of movement a day. In the first class he is concerned solely with functional movement, the articulation of the whole body. In the second class he is concerned with putting this armory of skills to creative use, learning to compose sequences of movement, exploring the relationship of dynamics, rhythm, design, motivation and gesture.

There are, according to Erich Fromm, four essentials for the professional approach to any art: discipline, concentration, patience and supreme concern. The first three provide the means of acquiring the necessary craft; the fourth can transform this into the realm of creative expression. Yet it is my experience over twenty years as a director in the theatre that in the training of the actor it is the vocal and the physical techniques that are most neglected. It is partly that the average length of two years is all too inadequate for the training of the actor, and partly that few actors continue their training thereafter either by working on themselves or by attending classes. Unlike the dancer who has to work remorselessly at his physical equipment or a singer at his voice, the actor, all too often, is able to get by on personality and charm, especially in the media of television and film.

Similarly in America one encounters in drama departments up and down the country a total lack of provision for the teaching of movement or voice. Too often, if they are provided, they are given by an actor or director who is all too patently himself in need of training, imposing upon a class of young students a series of ad hoc, haphazardly chosen exercises, ranging from Grotowski to Graham, out of context, ill-digested, and without any relevance to the needs of the individual student -- and often without any preliminary warm-up. The blind indeed lead the blind.

One has only to watch an average movement class to observe how the same set of exercises produces quite different results from different people. Each student in the class will think that he is doing the same exercise as his fellows without realizing that anything is wrong. We so automatically assume that movement is natural to man that we find it difficult even to acknowledge that we know nothing of the muscular movements required for even so simple an act as sitting down. As Sir Charles Sherrington, the great pioneer in modern study of the nervous system, and a Nobel Prize winner, observes in his book, The Endeavour of Jean Fernel:

> It is largely the reflex element in the willed movement
> or posture which, by reason of its unconscious character,
> defeats our attempts to know the 'how' of the doing of even

a willed act. Breathing, standing, walking, sitting, although innate, along with our growth, are apt, as movements, to suffer from defects in our ways of doing them.
A chair unsuited to a child can quickly induce special and
bad habits of sitting, and of breathing. In urbanized and
industrialized communities bad habits in our motor acts
are especially common. But verbal instruction as to how
to correct wrong habits of movement and posture is very
difficult. The scantiness of our sensory perception of how
we do them makes it so. The faults tend to escape our direct observation and recognition. Of the proprioceptive
reflexes as such, whether of muscle or ear (vestibule),
we are unconscious. We have no direct perception of the
"wash" of the labyrinthine fluid, or, indeed, of the exist-
ence of the labyrinths at all. In their case subjective projection, instead of indicating, blinds the place of their
objective source. Correcting the movements carried out
by our proprioceptive reflexes is something like trying
to reset a machine, whose works are intangible, and the
net output all we know of the running. Instruction in such
an act has to fall back on other factors more accessible
to sense; thus, in skating, to "feeling" that edge of the
skate-blade on which the movement bears. To watch another performer trying the movement can be helpful; or
a looking-glass in which to watch ourselves trying it.
The mirror can tell us often more than can the most pain-
staking attempt to "introspect." F. Mathias Alexander
has done a service to the subject by insistently treating
each act as involving the whole integrated individual, the
whole psycho-physical man. To take a step is an affair,
not of this or that limb solely, but of the total neuro-mus-
cular activity of the moment -- not least of the head and
the neck.

The Alexander Technique to which Sir Charles Sherrington
refers is, to my mind, integral to the training of the actor, singer
or dancer. And especially to the average actor. Look at any gather-
ing of actors and observe the rounded shoulders of one; the heavy,
over-emphatic movement of another; here one shoulder higher than
the other; there a head jerked back, chin stuck out, or a clumsy
awkward walk, or protruding stomach, and the many other manifestations of what Mathias Alexander described as the bad use of the
self, all manifestations of muscular tension, acquired through bad
habits over the years, leading in due course and all too often to a
slipped disc, backache, fatigue, depression, etc.
    Yet none of this is at all necessary. Professor Frank Pierce
Jones, at Tufts University's Institute for Psychological Research,

has observed how in small children, of two to three years of age, the seemingly effortless and tireless energy of these children stems from the fact that in them the proper relationship between head, neck and back is still maintained, "so that there is a perfect balance thoughout the organism, so that every action is performed with the minimum of strain and tension. But when the relationship is interfered with, the balance is destroyed, and strain and compensating tensions are multiplied. For example, when a small child stoops to pick up something he moves down smoothly, with the weight of his body in equilibrium throughout the movement, which can be reversed at any time without a jerk. An adult performing the same movement loses equilibrium at the start and preserves his balance by increasing tension, often to such a degree that he is pulled up on his toes to keep him from falling over."

The main problem in re-educating people in the correct use of themselves is, as Alexander always saw it, that we have all become so accustomed to our usual way of doing things that it "feels right" to us. So that any more efficient way of doing things is bound, at first anyway, to "feel wrong." And there is, also, the fact that the Alexander Technique can be imparted only through experience. It is, as Aldous Huxley described it, one of the non-verbal humanities. The Technique is not a matter of doing certain exercises, or of osteopathi manipulation; and although one of its effects is to lengthen and strengt en the spine (often adding a quarter to half an inch to the height of a person), it has nothing to do with sitting with a straight back and keep ing one's head up. Nor is it a question of finding a correct posture. It is rather a question of one's whole bearing, so that one has absolut control over whatever one is doing, whether it is gardening, driving, playing golf, sitting, singing, and so on. To the degree to which the student learns not to intrude any of his old habits, and submits himself to the manual guidance of the teacher, acquiring thereby a felt knowledge, he receives a new sensory experience. As a consequence of this re-education his neck feels free, his head feels as if it is going forward and up, and his torso feels as if it is lengthening. He will emerge, as Clifford Turner who taught voice at the Royal Academ of Dramatic Art once described it to me, "feeling ten feet tall." The major results of this training are an overall flexibility and ease of movement, less tension in the jaw, more relaxation in the tongue and throat, and deeper breathing because of the new alignment in the diaphragm. There is also a sense of weightlessness and a lessening of the amount of effort previously thought necessary to move one's limbs

This lighter-than-air effect should not be confused with what is customarily meant by relaxation, a complete letting go of the body. It is rather the relaxation of the panther, able to spring into action at any moment. As to breathing, Alexander was concerned to coax an awareness of breathing as it supports movement, and of movement as it supports breathing. The possibilities of orchestration between the two, in activity, are practically infinite. "We never talk about breathing," Alexander once informed a pupil, thus expressing his concern that it should be seen only as a function of using oneself properly.

Joyce Warrack, who for many years taught in the Opera School at the Royal College of Music, and applied Alexander's principles to the teaching of singing, has drawn attention to some remarks of Vincenzo Vannini in his book, Della Voce Umana, published in Florence in 1924. "Nature's means are essentially simple, it is only we who complicate matters with our pretentious attempts to be helpful. All that the singer can do is to remain a spectator. He must cease to interfere and rather cultivate an attitude of intelligent laziness ... Nature has no need of our assistance; leave the diaphragm to do its own work; neither help nor hinder it but leave it alone. There is no need of special methods of breath control for singing. Nor is there any lack of breath in the normally healthy human being." Vannini considered singing as only slightly different from declamation or reading aloud. "It is a question of degree and getting accustomed to it. Once the new habit has been formed Nature imposes no obstacles."

As Joyce Warrack observes (The Alexander Journal 1964; Spring issue): "It will be found that the Alexander Technique, designed to induce the best possible relationship between the head, neck, torso and legs at any given moment, will make for an unconstricted throat and freedom for the lungs and thorax. It is interesting, too, to think in terms of the circulation of the breath, with varying force according to demand, rather than of storing it up and squeezing it out like toothpaste."

Almost all teachers experience the frustration of working with students whose tensions seem so much part of their "character" that nothing can be done with them. Further progress seems impeded. Joyce Wodeman, formerly principal teacher of drama at the Royal College of Music, who was my first Alexander teacher, and who now teaches the technique full time at the Royal Academy of Dramatic Art, has recorded how the Alexander Technique is capable of freeing the student of these problems of fundamental rigidity and tension.

"What form does 'bad use' normally take in my students? And how does it affect their acting? Basically, of course, it takes the same form as in all of us -- pulling back the head, pulling in the back, hunching the shoulders, stiffening the arms and legs and so on. These habits are harmful to everyone, but they can be a part handicap to an opera singer or actor."

She records how, with the Technique, the students undoubtedly become more teachable, "more able to take in what one is saying, more able to accept criticism without feeling that they have 'failed' abyssmally when told they are doing something wrong. The main reason for this is, I think, that lessons in the technique shift one's centre of concern from trying to be 'right' to thinking of all one's activity as a process that has become ill-directed in some respects, but can be put right by conscious re-direction. The change of attitude in students is often very marked; from being over-confident or over-anxious, they come to accept more humbly the fact that we are all at fault in our different ways, but have it in our power to change if we are ready to be objective towards ourselves.

"As a first step this must involve learning how to stop doing the familiar thing (which feels right because it is so familiar that it is no longer conscious) in order to experiment with and experience something new. This realization that one can always inhibit and re-direct brings a sense of security; what fundamentally makes for fear of criticism and discouragement in all walks of life, I am sure, is the pernicious idea that 'being right' is the only criterion and that if one is 'wrong' one has flopped as a human being! Of course, the technique cannot make a good singer, actor, dancer out of someone who does not possess the necessary talent. What it can do, and often strikingly, is to awaken the student to how he is strangling his natural capacity and provide him with the means whereby to stop doing so."

THE CARE AND FEEDING OF DINOSAURS

PAUL BARRY

This work is about acting, and I must admit that I begin it with some trepidation. There are many splendid books and articles about the actor's art, inspirational tomes that read like Thomas Aquinas or Kahlil Gibran, as well as maddeningly simplistic (but necessary) instructions in cheating and upstage turns and timing off the crests of laughs. There are books on acting written by actors and books on directing written by directors. There are books by Konstantin Stanislavsky and Michael Chekhov and the Roberts Brustein and Benedetti and the Richards Boleslavsky, Schechner and Brown.

Unfortunately, there are no books on acting by Vince Lombardi or Paul "Bear"Bryant. I hope to demonstrate the need for such an athletic approach to this art of acting here.

But first: If I am to write about acting and actors, I must begin by saying that I believe the actor and his art cannot be separated from the kind of theatre in which he works. I am concerned with the actor who performs in the plays of the great playwrights before living audiences -- acting, to me, on its highest level. An actor whose fondest dreams center on collecting handsome residuals from huckstering toilet paper or droning out mindless drivel on television soap operas has little to gain from me, and there is little that I need to give to him.

The highest purpose of the actor is to cooperate with the other artists of the theatre in mirroring the totality of human experience. Theater must relate to and serve its audience, but not pander to it. Theatre must satisfy the emotional, visceral needs of that audience as well as appeal to its higher motives. Finally, theatre must entertain without sacrificing its artistic integrity.

The question of whether a play is worth doing or not is disputable, difficult to answer, subject to judgments of individual taste. I am hard put for rules, and only a vast knowledge of the world repertoire, combined with instinct and taste, can supply one with sufficient criteria for judgment. We can hint at some rules, of course, though each has a multitude of exceptions. There are mimetic plays in which purely aesthetic purposes are achieved: universal emotional needs are satisfied vicariously. We may say that the more universal those needs, and the more fully they are satisfied, the better the play. (Our Town or Under Milk Wood describes everyone's town; Peyton Place does not.) Didactic plays inspire specific action as well. (The Crucible fought McCarthyism.) The over-all value of a play can only be judged by stabs at a scale that puts Hamlet on one end and the toilet paper commercial on the other end. Hamlet, when its requirements are fulfilled, is the crowning theatre experience for artists and audience alike; the toilet paper commercial, if it works, does nothing more or less than motivate the audience to buy one brand rather than another.

THE PERFORMANCE CONTRACT

Assuming, then, the availability of a play worth doing, theatre practitioners must begin with a consideration of the basic nature of the human animal and that creature's need for theatre. Need? Yes. Theatre exists because of the needs of the audience. Inhibited from giving full rein to such instincts as sex, violence and territorial possession by societal strictures, the human animal seeks alleviation of his frustrations through his highly developed powers of imagination, through dreams, fantasies and vicarious experiences.

Throughout man's history, theatre, in some form, has been present -- from ritual religious sacrificial rites to medieval morality plays, Elizabethan masques, more modern vaudeville. Today's dramas are the sophisticated, sensitive outgrowths of centuries of attempts at answering basic needs. Tomorrow may bring an even better way.

The performance contract, then, is a phenomenon dependent upon the relationship between two groups of humans: audience (with emotional needs) and actors (ready to minister to those needs). Other unseen theatre practitioners are, of course, involved: playwrights, designers, directors, technicians. Yet theatre depends primarily upon the exchange between those individuals attending and those performing the play.

The actors are paid for their service, not only in coin of the realm, but in emotional currency as well. If they, as artists, have fulfilled their function and moved the audience to laughter and tears, applause and cheers, then they are doubly paid for their concentrated efforts and experience their own need fulfillments as well. The phenomenon of living theatre is the epitome of social intercourse, an intimate kinetic emotional exchange, infinitely complicated, geometrically complex, though based in biological simplicity.

This exquisite phenomena happens to two groups of human animals packed compactly into a single space. The phenomena depends on the living, breathing presence of both groups. They cannot be removed from each other in time and place without reducing the phenomena to a sterile and bankrupt imitation of itself. *

How does the performance contract, this exquisite phenomena, operate? One must first realize that the audience member is capable of reacting physiologically to a fictional experience (theatre) as if it were a real experience. Because the actor and the audience member are of the same species, it follows that all participants in the performance experience are capable of converting the artificial dramatic situation to physiological reality through imagination. There are limitations, of course, and we can waste a great deal of time discussing the possibility of absolutes, but our dramatic traditions over the last century or so have emphasized the necessity of the appearance of absolute reality, and we, as theatre artists, have profited by this standard, whether we are capable of achieving it or not. To simplify matters and to save time and paper, I will postulate the following: the more believable the performance, the more likely it will satisfy the emotional needs of the audience.

The actor progresses to the ultimate in emotional commitment (and believability) from a neutral point, his awareness of himself and his own reality, through a series of steps. He reads the play, identifies the character, examines the character, rehearses the play point by point, absorbing the character's moods, assumes the physical (including vocal) characteristics of the character, defines emotionally the character's relationships to his environment and the other characters in the play, and, finally, in performance, through concentration, eliminates everything but the character's immediate concerns from his mind.

The audience member begins from a similarly neutral point: he buys his ticket and arrives at his seat, agreeing to physically remove himself from the concrete concerns of his real world. As the (successful) play unfolds, he progresses from curiousity to interest to sympathy to empathy. The greater the emotional similarity between the observer and character, the greater the identification and the more complete the empathetic response. If the play succeeds, the audience member might laugh, though in truth, he came into the theatre an unhappy man; he might cry, though in truth the sorrow and the loss are not his; he may experience arousal and alleviation of a dozen basic instincts, sex, aggression, dominance, greed, parenthood, religion, patriotism, etc., all through actual physiological responses to fictional but believable stimuli.

In African Genesis, Robert Ardrey describes the performance contract in another way when he defines our uninhibited observer as "an audience reduced by darkness and anonymity and a kind of hypnosis to a group of reacting organisms in whom ethical, moral, virtuous

* Live theatre vs. film is a separate question, too long and complex to go into here. I said at the outset I'm concerned with the legitimate, classic (if you will) actor. You'll just have to accept this prejudice.

or thoughtful considerations play a limited part. It cannot be said that [the playwright] writes for primitive man. What he writes for, rather, is contemporary man in a most stripped-down, uninhibited, unself-conscious moment of his nature."

The actor and the audience member arrive at the height of the emotional experience together, supporting each other each step of the way, each moment of the play. The actor, as the character, says something funny; the audience member laughs. The actor, as the character, shows grief; the audience member sighs. The character "dies" and the audience member weeps. All of the sounds of the theatre auditorium, laughs, sobs, sighs, the clicking of purse snaps, the shuffling of feet, the creak of the seats, spontaneous applause, whispers, all feed the actor, forcing his concentration, subtly altering his performance. The effect is cumulative and reciprocal. A good performance is supported progressively by the audience, and a bad performance is diminished by the audience as they become more and more restless, unsatisfied and bored. *

EMOTION

The actor's basic talent, then, would seem to be his ability to react with conviction to an imagined or artificial stimulus. Romeo is told by Bathazar that Juliet is dead. In order for the audience to experience the vicarious effect, in order for them to empathize with Romeo, they must, individually and in concert, believe his sorrow. They must believe, in their willful suspension of disbelief, that both the death of Juliet and the sorrow of Romeo are true occurrences, that they are observing the true effect of these occurrences in Romeo's emotional reaction to the news.

What is emotionality? It is a behavioral trait that appears to be connected anatomically with the diencephalic section of the forebrain and physiologically with the circulation of the blood. Emotion (e-motion), etymologically defined, is a form of motion. It cannot exist without movement. A static state is a lack of motion, and an organism at rest is one lacking in emotion. In physics, motion is defined as heat. On the orgasmic level, we may define emotion in terms of the movement of an animal. Indeed, the emotion itself and its manifestation in the movement of the creature are virtually inseparable. Do we run because we are afraid, or are we afraid because we run?

* Both the actor's and the audience member's emotional experience relies upon imagination, which depends largely upon concentration, which in turn depends upon freedom from distraction. The wise producer is aware that a theatre must be a special place: correctly heated or cooled, with proper acoustics, seats well-tiered, elimination of unwanted light and sound, etc. But this is a bit of a digression. I refer you to Stratford, Ontario, for the well designed theatre plant if you are interested.

This may at first be difficult to accept. Yet though most of us would be hard put to describe the physiological manifestations of any given emotion, we nevertheless can recognize these emotions. All species "speak" a body language, a form of communication much older and more reliable, indeed far more "honest" than verbal language. The human animal speaks a body language that varies in its subtleties from one culture to another, yet still remains universal in its manifestation of basic emotions.

Although an American may signify "yes" by nodding his head up and down, and an Arab may use the same motion to say "no," they will react alike to danger, to sexual stimulus, to food, etc. Basic emotions have to do with instinctual responses to appropriate stimuli. The older the instinct, the more likely the similarity of response among different species and/or subgroups of the same species. Given a state of hunger, for instance, all humans will react alike physiologically to the sight and smells of a banquet table laden with food. The sight and smell of it creates a feeling of weakness. The stomach churns, bodily tension is increased, the salivary glands are activated.

Again, though we may be intellectually unable to define or to verbally describe the physical manifestations of an emotion, nevertheless, we are intuitively capable of recognizing them when we see them. Further, considering the amazing complexity of the human organism, no emotional reaction exists in isolation. The stronger the emotion, and the more active its physiological manifestation, the more likely that the entire organism will be influenced.

Simply stated, we can tell the emotional state of another human being merely by observing his movements. If he is angry, he will be tense, probably loud, move rapidly and talk quickly; if he is tired, he will be slow and lethargic; if he is sad, he may cry. Of course, there's a catch: if he knows we're watching, he'll be inclined to inhibit his actions, to hide his true feelings. To complicate matters, our own cultural conditioning has taught us to be guarded in our observation of others. To stare at another human being, especially one caught up in the agonies of an extreme emotional experience, is considered bad manners in most civilized societies.

However, what if we were to observe our subject from a hidden vantage point, a peephole, or crack in the door? What if our curiosity had led us to watch and listen carefully, to concentrate on the unsuspecting victim without fear of his discovering us? Then, we could be certain of his emotional state, indeed, of his whole emotional make-up, by the movements of his body and the sounds he makes. Not only would we be able to intuitively define his emotional state, but we would also participate vicariously in his emotionality.

The theatre, of course, gives us our peephole, our vantage point. The performance contract frees us from our normal inhibitions and allows us to watch (or to do, if we are the actors) without fear of discovery or social censure. Just as we are able to identify with a human being in the throes of real agony, so too does our identification with the actor depend upon his ability to react with accuracy to the imagined or artificial stimulus. If the text says Juliet is dead, and yet Romeo's movements and sounds do not corroborate this fact (or fiction), then the audience knows intuitively that something is wrong. They are deprived of the possibility of complete identification, and they must conclude that Romeo is, in truth, not Romeo at all, but merely a bad actor. The performance experience is aborted, the play crumbles, and the audience member ruminates over thoughts of tar and feathers.

Clear so far? An uninhibited observer, free of distractions, and a concentrated, believable, also uninhibited performer. But there are still a few more catches.

DISTAL AND PROXIMAL

Studies on kinesis have shown us how distance can be an important factor in interpreting the intentions of another member of our species. We unconsciously define private territories and respond emotionally as others approach or impinge upon that territory. Since basic emotional audience needs depend upon the invasion of private space, the degree of proximity, the distance of another's body from our own, defines both threat and intention qualitatively and quantitatively. Seldom do we experience intense emotional involvement with another directly from a distance. Except in the theatre.

The actor must be capable of not only reacting with complete believability to the artificial stimulus, he must be capable of projecting his emotional states over distances. Moreover, he must be capable of compromise without loss. He must convince the customer in the back row while simultaneously convincing the customer in the front row, though they might be separated by some two hundred feet of distance. The actor must, therefore, have a voice that can project not only the clarity of the text, the playwright's words, but also the emotional state of the character without forcing or shouting or tearing up his vocal chords. He must be able to play the customary eight performances a week without fear of laryngitis.

In addition, he must have a body capable of reacting freely and completely to the emotional impulses of the line of the play. This ability is harder to define, and its development is too often ignored in the normal course of actor training, but body training is every bit as important, perhaps even more so, than voice training for the actor. An actor who does not move freely, who is stiff, lacking in balance, inhibited in his movements, gesture-conscious, ungraceful, who gives a weak or clumsy appearance, cannot be said to be a good actor. With more than a little help from an army of technicians, he may be able to get away with a small voice and weak body for television, film or radio performances, but he is doomed to failure on the living stage.

There is one more element that is a function of the actor's body and voice, and that is energy. The actor must be able to hold the audience's attention and interest, and maintain his own intense concentration, throughout the two to three hours' duration of the performance. (Again, eight times a week.) He must be able to go the distance, conveying not only believability but also excitement throughout the entire play. He cannot succumb to fatigue, and his survival in the theatre can well depend upon his reliability. An actor who develops a reputation for missing performances because of periodic illness will soon find himself unemployable.

THE ACTOR'S PREPARATION

Aside from the grueling business of marketing himself, the round-making and showcasing and the endless sending of pictures and resumes and the interviews and auditions, the actor's preparation can be divided into four areas. They are:

1. The instrument: the development of the actor's body and voice.
2. Skills and techniques: role preparation, sensory training, rehearsal procedures.
3. Education: history of the theatre; styles; relationship of actor to playwrights, directors, designers; the study of the vast repertoire of the world's dramatic literature.
4. Experience: both in rehearsal and performance before live audiences.

Ideally, an actor training program would involve all of these elements, nurturing the actor's talent through a balanced development. Unfortunately, time and money often prohibit such a complete program, and the prejudices and limitation of teachers impose a more subtle limitation.

Of course all of the above is pretty useless unless it's in the hands of native talent and sometimes useless even then, for (very rarely) talent and instinct need little instruction. (Who taught Marlon Brando what it was that allowed his Stanley Kowalski to exist?) Throughout, I assume the presence of talent, without which no words are useful. (Do not ask me to define talent; it can't be done.)

WHERE TO BEGIN

Theoretically, the actor should already be possessed of the emotional equipment he needs to draw his audience into the vicarious experience. He speaks the same verbal and non-verbal language; he is of the same species, subject to the same instincts. However, as a young adult, he has already been trained and conditioned away from the actor's ideal of uninhibited emotional response. The very social conditioning, the culturalization that makes the theatre a necessity for the audience, has also served to suppress and inhibit the actor. He has been taught to hide his emotions, to suppress his tears, his cries and his laughter. He has been told to fold his hands, to hide his yawn, to apologize for his belches and to avoid public displays of affection or anger. In short, a goodly portion of the business of growing up in modern society is given to learning a vocabulary of emotional euphemisms, all designed to soften or hide true feelings.

In most of the acting classes that I have participated in or observed, a great deal of time has been spent in an effort to effect a kind of emotional reversal to restore the actor to the capacity for simple uninhibited response he was capable of as a three-year-old.

It can be argued that the ability to combine character identification with uninhibited emotional response is the essence of the actor's talent. An actor can do it. A non-actor can't.

Experience, especially under relatively non-pressured rehearsal circumstances, working with good directors and veteran actors, can serve to improve the student actor's capacity to give himself freely to the performance, reducing his inhibitions. Just as he has learned the language of social euphemisms from his peers, parents and teachers, so he re-learns his childhood emotional freedoms from his new theatre peers and directors. It is in this respect that repertory apprenticeship is most valuable, though there is still danger of forcing the emerging ability. (That is, the necessity of opening on a certain date whether the apprentice is ready or not can lead to false performances.)

THE CHOICE

As in all human endeavors, the development of the actor is subject to the battle between expedience and patience. A trusted friend and teacher of acting once stated to me that he believed he could teach anyone to act, given enough time. How much? Ten years? Three? Fifty? Twenty?

Because it could take a human being an entire lifetime to perfect the actors' craft, I have chosen to concentrate, in training the actor, on the development of the instrument. In making this choice, I make no contrary judgments about the importance of skills, education or experience. All are important, but priorities must be observed

In concentrating on the instrument, I must assume at least the possibility of that intangible called talent. I believe I can subject both the actor and the non-actor to my system of training over a period of time. At the end of that period, I will have improved the general condition of both. They both will be sleeping better, eating better, and both will probably be easier to live with. They'll both look better in a bathing suit. The actor will be a far better actor. The non-actor will still be a non-actor.

THE INSTRUMENT

A talented violinist can produce better music from a $10,000 Stradivarius than he can from a $65 pawn-shop special. The actor is both artist and instrument. The fulfillment of his talent depends upon the physical condition of his body and his ability to use that body.

I have pointed out that cultural conditioning serves to inhibit free expression of emotion. Such a process makes its mark upon the anatomy as well. Any inhibiting process will create bodily tensions, ultimately resulting in muscular rigidity, both in internal and skeletal systems. Constant social pressures, especially among city dwellers, make relaxation and easy sleep difficult, if not impossible. Any deviation from social norms complicates the process, adding the regulatory guilt factor. We grow to young adulthood stiff, tense, unable to relax; when we do react to emotional stimuli, our bodily tensions cause us to react spastically, jerkily. We gesture cautiously, the gesture carrying the whole body along.

Our over-mechanized society with its heavy emphasis on motorized transportation robs us of exercise not only for the muscles of the feet, legs and lower body, but also for the pulmonary and cardiovascular systems. Under-developed gluteus maximus muscles make additional demands on the abdominal muscles in maintaining posture, thus depriving the diaphragm of proper, natural support and control. Speech is inhibited, and the voice is underdeveloped while the lungs receive less oxygen per breath than they need.

Bad eating habits, paradoxically a common thing in the richest nation in the world, contribute to general bad health, and diets heavy in animal fats and carbohydrates combine with a lack of exercise to produce a condition of overweight. Better than 55 million Americans are at least 20 pounds overweight. That's more than a quarter of the entire population. Heavy smoking and an overdependence on drugs complicate the problems further.

Other subtle elements tend to work against the actor. Early in high school, there is a tendency for students to polarize their interests. The "sensititive" intellectual students gravitate toward the arts, and the more physical students involve themselves in competitive sports. Pro-artistic comesto mean anti-jock. By the time personality traits have solidified in young adulthood, the incipient actor virtually glories in his inability to do anything more physical than climb the steps to his cold-water flat.

And yet we have seen that the actor's instrument must respond directly to the emotional impulse. It must function efficiently with no wasted motions. Its movements must be specific, stating from moment to moment the context of the play. It must have balance and grace. It must be capable of sustained effort, impervious to fatigue. It must contain a loud, resonant and flexible vocal instrument. It must be capable of combat, with or without weapons. It must be aesthetically pleasing to the eye. It must be capable of experiencing sensory stimuli fully.

EMOTIONAL CAPACITY

Let's begin with emotion. It has been stated that, physiologically, emotion is directly related to the circulation of the blood. It naturally follows that bad circulation dulls emotional response. Bad circulation is a symptom of an inefficient cardiovascular system and is further complicated by cholesterol build-up in the veins and arteries. The actor can sharpen his sensory perception and heighten his emotional capacity by reducing his intake of animal fats and improving the function of his heart and lungs. Sounds too simple? It isn't. It takes a lot of will power.

OXYGEN

The actor needs oxygen for two purposes, energy and voice. Singing and speaking in the theatre require more air than normal conversation. Less obvious is the body's need of oxygen for an energetic sustained performance. Any physical activity requires energy; the body produces energy by burning foodstuffs, and oxygen is the burning agent. The body can store food, but it can't store oxygen, and in badly conditioned bodies, the means for delivering the oxygen from the lungs to the muscles is weak and limited. As increased activity demands more energy, the system is taxed, and, oxygen demand can quickly surpass the body's capacity to produce it. When this occurs, we experience a depressing, weak feeling that we call fatigue. For any given activity, the energy requirements are comparable for each individual, with minor variations for body size and overall health. The difference between good and bad physical condition lies in the body's capacity to absorb and utilize oxygen; good physical condition can be both measured and expressed in terms of endurance.

In recent years extensive studies have been conducted by the United States Air Force to determine how endurance may be increased and over-all health thereby improved. Literally thousands of Air Force personnel were trained and tested, and the results were documented by Dr. Kenneth Cooper in _Aerobics_, a book that should be required reading for every student actor in the country. Briefly stated, Dr. Cooper describes how endurance levels can be increased by a progressive schedule involving exercises that force the body to process more and more oxygen, namely running, bicycling, swimming or sports that involve continuous running -- e.g., handball, squash, basketball, etc. Lung efficiency can be improved and maintained by anyone who can build his endurance up to a point where he can run six miles a week at a speed under eight minutes per mile or swim six hundred yards at a speed under fifteen minutes six days a week or ride a bicycle thirty miles per week at a speed over fifteen miles per hour (five miles in twenty minutes, six days a week.) These are minimum exercise requirements for maintaining good conditioning; any increase in distances or improvement in elapsed time cannot help but put the actor way ahead of his more sedentary fellows.

Not only does this type of exercise increase the efficiency of the lungs, it also strengthens the heart, and, in turn, the entire system of veins and arteries. It improves the tone of the internal and external muscles. It toughens the body without inordinate weight loss, except for those who are overweight. It improves the body's capacity to resist infection and disease as well as the efficiency of the digestive system. It makes it possible for the body to relax with greater ease; sleep is sounder, the body thereby derives more rest from less time sleeping.

Although aerobic exercises are not a cure-all for the actor or anyone else, they are incomparable in terms of the amount of benefit per time invested.

STRENGTH

Any sport, if actively pursued, will build strength and improve the appearance of the body. If a person is underweight, an increased protein intake, together with graduated weight-lifting, will add muscle to the body. However, weight-lifting should always be combined with stretches and limbering exercises as well as aerobics to insure against muscle tightness or shortening of the muscle fibre.

THE ACTOR'S EXERCISES

Over the last ten years, I have evolved a system of movement training specifically for the stage actor, borrowing exercises from ballet and modern dance, judo, yoga and singing-voice training. The approach is strictly physical, though its application is ultimately dependent on the actor's innate talent.

I have attempted several times to describe these exercises on paper, but I find it both difficult and tedious to write about them. Moreover, the exercises evolve, changing subtly in emphasis with each new class that comes before me. One thing I do know, and it is something of a sad realization: little can be accomplished in a summer season or a semester or even a school year. This kind of training is an ongoing process, one that must be compared to the training of the dancer or the musician. Eventually, the actor might be able to give the class to himself, and, hopefully, after several years of training, he will have developed the discipline to do so.

I seem to be the only teacher teaching my kind of class, but the actor can derive similar benefits by studying ballet, modern dance, judo and voice. However, each of these disciplines has other objectives, separate from the development of the actor's instrument.

If the student actor buys the premises that I have written of here, he is invited to apply for a place in my company and to work with me. I cannot write down what I do -- I can only teach it to the actor's body, not his brain, not his intellectual or critical capacity, but his body, his instrument. Even then, he must develop an all-important, sadly rare virtue: patience. It takes a long time to become a great artist, and patience alone makes it possible to disregard the turning leaves of the calendar. Impatience and arbitrary time goals ("If I don't make it big within five years, I'll look for another way to make a living"), have destroyed more potentially fine actors than any other factor. If the actor allows himself to keep alive any other options, any other life choice, he will never make it in today's theatre.

THE MIRROR COMPANY, DÖPPELGANGING, DNA AND THE REPRODUCTIVE PROCESS

KELLY YEATON

We have run across an unusual theatrical production structure, with some related techniques of training, development and insight which may be specially applicable to certain problems of continuous production and of repertory, as well as to experimental productions of many kinds. Essentially it is the use of double companies in a special manner, which we now call mirror companies ... double casts which are mirror images of each other, two actors for each role. We have explored the idea far enough to say that the method is surprising, flexible, subtle and has some peculiar qualities of its own. I hope that some skeptic will investigate and will report what <u>he</u> finds in the method.

EARLY WARNINGS

Directors, like many other artists, often arrive at a clear consciousness of their own work only by looking backward, trying to understand and analyze their more successful intuitive actions. Some thirty years ago a young actress friend named Laura happened to say that <u>she</u> had always imagined <u>Glass Menagerie</u> with Laura as the central role. Having met Williams in St. Louis when his name was Tom, I was aware that he might well imagine Tom as the central role, but when I saw Laurette Taylor play it, Amanda was plainly the central role. Yet, when the Gentleman Caller tells the story to some friend in later years, will he not tell it as if he were the central character? Doesn't every actor play his role as if it were the center of the story? Do we not all see ourselves as central to the story of our own experience?

When I came to cast <u>Menagerie</u> for the arena I announced a six-person company, rather than a single cast. The show was to play for six week-ends, twelve performances, and I privately told each member of the company that they would have an opportunity to play

73

both roles at least once during the run. The girls would play both Amanda and Laura and the boys both Tom and the Caller. When not on stage they would be in the booth, controlling lights and sound. We rehearsed for three weeks in the spring, broke for summer vacation, and finished with three more weeks in the fall.

It wasn't the best performance in the world, but it maintained a balance that most Menageries sadly miss. Night after night we came down the center of the road of the play, never swerving from the heart that is Truth ... "nothing in excess" ... a true ensemble. Looking backward I tried to think what caused that curious creative excitement that we had had in rehearsal. Partly it had been that we were always playing the play, not just a role, "my role." That self-centeredness is the cause of many kinds of creative blindness. I now think that the principle of shared possession of the roles had helped us. There were three versions of Laura ... Laura/Dianne, Laura/Sonya and Laura/Francine ... but the three agreed on the central image of Laura-of-the-play. And the role was a frame in which we could see each of the actresses with their personal and unique qualities.

Actors have mixed reactions about any system in which the director makes a less-than-total commitment. The Menagerie company was a happy one because they were getting to play two roles, but the reaction to finding that a role is to be played by another person is one of threat and of competition. The element of "being selected" is a vital one in ensemble dynamics, and so is the sense of personal possession of a role. But in mirror companies there are other rewards. They have company in their task, someone who can understand the problems and the challenges of the role. Actors can and do learn to cooperate and to compete and also to be supportive of each other. In a way, each player is an acting coach or assistant director for the other.

DOUBLE KNACK

In the next few years I occasionally double-cast a role, often used expert actors as creative understudies in rehearsal, and regularly spent a serious amount of time in the development of understudies. None of this activity gave me any foreshadowing of the explosive development that occurred when we went into rehearsals with a double company of The Knack. The play obviously required training and skill in improvisation, and I was aware that a four-person group doesn't work as richly in this medium as does an eight-person group. (I think the "critical mass" may be five or six.) Anyway, we had two weeks to play; I selected two complete casts and announced that my primary aim was the deliberate creation of an ensemble, that one cast would play one week and the other would play the second week, and that these separate casts would be matched and selected later ... meanwhile we were to work as an ensemble for a few weeks. As it turned out, it was an exciting, happy and stimulating time. During warm-ups we did a lot of mirror work, often to music, and naturally the actors tended to pair off with the other actor assigned to the same role. They learned a deep identification with each other and, in the mirror rehearsals, with the role-image the other actor was developing.

MIRROR METHODS

We worked largely in a relationship that we called cross-mirror in which the right hand of the Image reflects the right hand of the Actor. (In a conventional mirror the right hand of the spectator becomes the left hand of the image.) This had the advantage of not reversing "handedness" so that the players did not have to develop unusual dexterity in their left hands to match the dexterity of the other's right hand. It also gave special advantage to our use of the symmetrical arena space in which we worked, for cross-mirror space does not have the imaginary mirror-plane cutting through it, making an impenetrable barrier. The virtual space of cross-mirror has only an imaginary axis, around which everything revolves. In cross-mirror you may circle around the other person, and as you pass behind him you are in the shadowing relationship used by dancers to pick up steps from the demonstration of the choreographer. ("Ready, girls? Now, with me ... one, two...") All of the mirror and shadow relationships require deep empathy with the body and face and spirit of the other actor, and we had the advantage of knowing enough to work for the level that Paul Sills called "mutuality," a state in which one actually loses the sense of initiative by sharing it with the other actor. At this stage each of them believes and feels that he is "following the lead" of the other person. At this level the "magnetic field" between them is as sensitive and subtle as a divining rod or a Ouija board. And, as in the tight disciplines of yoga, the physical exercise becomes a pathway into the mind and feelings.

In a double company certain responses are natural and inevitable. Each actor watches his own opposite number with a special kind of perception and identification. When one cast is on stage the other cast watches, very personally. We encouraged this natural identification, and suggested constant physical shadowing and mirroring to assist this identification; we also suggested that, when they could, they should silently speak the words of the speeches -- a kind of private off-stage rehearsal process for the muscles and mind. It is a high-speed memorization method, but that wasn't mentioned. In these early stages, the actors on stage were carrying books, of course, while the circle of mirrors and shadows were working directly from the bodies and sounds of the working cast, with no need to bother with a book in hand.

After physical mirroring we jumped to a whole new game --

emotional reflections. (I remembered that the task of a non-directive therapist is chiefly to reflect back to his client his emotional tones -- like a selective mirror.) The outer ring was told to disregard the actual physical postures and actions and to feel for the inner "psychological gesture," the abstract posture or action that best expressed the feelings of the character at the moment -- piercing, caressing, retreating, fleeing, exploring.

Then we suggested the playing of "opposites," the inner inhibited action of the subtext -- the fear and insecurity concealed under Tolen's machismo and bragging, the sexual interest underlying Nancy's defensiveness, the violence and lewdness underlying Colin's shyness, etc. This was the exercise that we called the Döppelganger, and it provided the actors with more information that we could absorb in several days of rehearsal, and more useful than hours of intellectual lecture or discussion. (One Tolen was seriously shocked to find that in what I had called a "little sex comedy" there were three violent rapes in the subtextual material. "Of course," I said "that concealed violence is what loads the laughs and makes them explosive.")

In the Döppelganger the actor is allowed to swing freely from the continuing action of the rehearsal and the physical mirroring of his own character; he may stick to mirror and shadow relationships, or explore emotional gestures, or subtextual actions and feelings, or opposites. Often they find themselves playing with the other Doppelgangers in small counter-plays. It is a rich, deep, experiential and non-verbal method of exploration, which literally bypasses most of the problems involved in language communication. I am sure it could be used with a company who had no common verbal language at all. It also tends to diminish the importance of the director as an authority figure although not as an interpretive guide and coach.

Actually the double Knack company worked as a mirror company only during the early weeks before the two companies split for separate simultaneous rehearsals, but the impression and sense of ensemble never left them. When the productions were over we began to realize what riches we had not even used -- a double company of four players contains the potential for 26 different casts, of which we had used only two, save in rehearsals.

DOUBLE SIMULTANEOUS FITZ

In an evening of experimental exercises and demonstrations called Theatre '68: New Forms and Events I tried the next stage of exploration. There is a charming two-person one-act play called Fitz written by Maxime Furlaud about two young people at the end of a summer affair, in which they play various imaginary games with each other as the dialogue progresses, including the sailing of a small sloop to a quiet harbor, in pure pantomime. With a double cast, I rehearsed this and played it in cross-mirror with both casts simultaneously on stage, even speaking in perfect synchronization. This may have been the most rigid frame a set of actors was ever locked into ... they could neither move nor speak without the simultaneous and instantaneous agreement of the counter-player, yet to the eye there was neither hesitation nor any lack of spontaneity in speech or movement. And the audience response was to the play itself, not to the method of performance. Indeed, the difficulty of the performance seemed to have become transparent. In a way, between the two girls who each played Fitz we seemed to see the character herself, reflected in the two mirrors of the actresses. The differences were those of the players, the agreement was the character, or the character image.

MIRROR COMPANY OF MAD MOTHER: THE WHOLE HOG

With all this background I then projected the full application of the mirror company to a difficult problem, Ann Jellicoe's early play called The Sport of My Mad Mother of which two different editions were known to exist. My hypothesis was that it was a fascinating problem and that the flexibility of the mirror company would give us an opportunity to explore it more widely, deeply and extensively than could be done by a conventional production. (It also put twice as many young actors to work, although the wildness of the venture plainly scared away most of the graduate professional acting trainees. Those who came with us had much to gain and little local "prestige" to lose ... one faculty member and one graduate student excepted.)

By this time we had developed some highly sophisticated methods of using the various mirror relationships, including the use of tape-mime rehearsals. We constantly worked on the structure of the play, dropping scenes from one edition and interpolating scenes from the other. Our company was enormously resilient, scarcely blinking when told that we had a whole new first act to run tonight. We lost a member of the company and replaced him without trauma and without discussion. We did some auditions with the new man, tentatively accepted him, and at rehearsal simply told him to "hook on" and learn the play as a mirror. I suppose there must have been some direction and instruction given, but most of his information came to him directly from the person of the other player in rehearsal, never verbalized at all.

The final edition of Mother was actually very close to the second version that Jellicoe had published, but in working through all the variations and changes that we did in rehearsals I think that we internally knew why we were using the sequence we finally chose. We never used the final scene that Jellicoe wrote, a rather Brechtian skit of childbirth. But we felt the need for a birth scene, and developed one that we could not have imagined with any other company structure.

We started with a rather naturalistic scene of labor and delivery (to "strong" for the intimacy of arena and the general lightness of the play) but eventually ended with an abstracted mime scene that incor-porated a rather dazzling sequence of elements from many rites of passage for a young girl -- birth, presentation, initiation, a debutan ball, and graduation.

Mad Mother may not have been a popular smash hit on camp but it was deeply satisfying to the ensemble and to the director. (I s a general report of what we had been doing to Miss Jellicoe who nev answered.) Meanwhile I retired from the field of action to consider what had been happening and to try to come to some understanding of it. So we have developed this rather peculiar tool for directors, wha is it good for? What are the sources of its unique powers? When sho it be used? How much skill does it require?

POWERS AND QUALITIES

Well, it cannot be used fully until the actors have spent quite a lot of time locked into the various mirror relationships with other and I believe the physical mirroring is the crucial one. Moreover, t aim of attaining "mutuality" elevates the exercise from a mere disp of physical dexterity and mimicry. The use of abstraction in the "ps chological gestures" and subtextual actions requires a creative inter tation and transformation and elevates the method still another step. However, even at the lowest level of direct, slavish, precise, accur ate imitation the method has some strange qualities and one of them is the ability to reproduce itself. I mentioned the ability of the com-pany to heal itself from the sudden loss of a member. I think it may have been the use of that phrase that provided my final insight into the mirror company -- its ability to reproduce itself.

DNA / DNA

The structure of the molecule of nucleic acid (DNA) is said t be similar to a mirrored spiral, a double helix. One may say in rou terms that the genetic code lies in the sequence that lies along the s ral, but that it duplicates itself by the mirroring principle, by attra ing and training a second cast, which could in turn duplicate itself. I a college community of some size one could image a company of The Fantasticks with a successful production reproducing itself and beco ing a local tradition. Upperclassmen would seek out freshmen and sophomores and train them by mirroring, use them as understudies and hand on the obligation of finding and training another replacemen What are the royalties for a production intended to run forever?

FINAL REFLECTION

The mirror is not only the archetypal symbol of the process of the theatre, but may also contain an essential secret of life, the ability to reproduce in precise duplicate the kind of life it actually is, without much loss and with little distortion.